Advance Praise for Da

"Alice McDowell writes with gentle discernment. Her words are a light and a balm."

PIR ZIA INAYAT KHAN, head of the Inayati Sufi Order and author of
Mingled Waters: Sufism & the Mystical Unity of Religions

"When one is venturing into unfamiliar territory, possessing a good map can make all the difference. *Dance of Light* is such a map. Equally inspiring and informative, it draws from a wide range of spiritual and religious traditions to reveal the underlying arc of the spiritual journey, as seen through the eyes of an experienced and compassionate guide."

JALAJA BONHEIM, Ph.D., author of
The Sacred Ego and Aphrodite's Daughters

"Alice McDowell is a trustworthy and honest guide for those embarking upon the spiritual journey and all the adventures and misadventures that one will encounter along the way. *Dance of Light* strips away the falsities, simplifies the unnecessary complexities, and gives numerous resources to light the way, and specifically *your* way, as benefits your own soul and psyche."

MEGHAN DON award-winning author,
*Meditations with Teresa of Avila: A Journey into the
Sacred and Feminine Courage.*

"Alice McDowell's book *Dance of Light* is a stunning exploration of the phases, pitfalls, challenges, and joys of the spiritual life. Written in a warm and genuine voice, Alice shares decades of study and practice, both as a student and a teacher, in the Christian, Sufi and Zen traditions. This book truly serves as a guide, as she expertly synthesizes ideas and beliefs from these seemingly disparate traditions. In Alice's hands, the philosophies and faiths are clearly defined, both for their individual beauty and offerings, and for the astonishing ways that they all over-lap. The book is a valuable and rare treasure trove of impactful quotes from the world's Eastern and Western spiritual writers, all of them illuminated by Alice's insights, ruminations, and hard-won experiences. Each chapter closes with reflections that will challenge readers to both stretch and realize the possibilities of their own seeking and journeying. What a useful and timely guide *Dance of Light* is, its pages giving a seasoned partner to guide readers' intricate steps, and to take them more joyfully into the mystery and the magic of the dance."

MAUREEN O'BRIEN, author of
What Was Lost: Seeking Refuge from the Psalms

"I would like to offer my heartfelt endorsement of *Dance of Light: Christian, Sufi, and Zen Steps to Spiritual Realization.* I will be ordering this text for "Mysticism: East and West," a course that I teach at Southern Methodist University, as soon as it becomes available. *Dance of Light* not only articulates a thoughtful and nuanced depiction of the stages of the mystical journey (drawing primarily upon Christian mysticism, the Zen Ox Herding pictures and Sufism), but it also offers helpful and practical spiritual guidance for those who are seeking to access the wisdom that can be gained from a balanced and energized examination of the mystical life. *Dance of Light* speaks to readers in clear and accessible language, and offers the distilled insights of McDowell's decades of teaching and research on comparative mysticism. I strongly recommend this lucid, engaging, and inspiring text, written by a seasoned, well-grounded guide who has herself plumbed the depths of several mystical traditions."

G. WILLIAM BARNARD, professor of religious studies,
Southern Methodist University,
author of *Exploring Worlds and Living Consciousness*

"Alice McDowell's fluent and full-bodied voice integrates stories and teachings from several spiritual traditions with her personal journey — and prompts honest, self-compassionate reflection on your own. In *Dance of Light*, she guides you though your experiences of renunciation, discouragement, self-satisfaction, renewal, awakening, or something without words. This book is inspirational material, lovely going!"

MARY GILLILAND, author of *Gathering Fire*
and *The Ruined Walled Castle Garden*

DANCE OF LIGHT

Minneapolis
SECOND EDITION December 2022

Dance of Light: Christian, Sufi and Zen wisdom
for today's spiritual seeker
Copyright © 2022 by Alice McDowell
All rights reserved.

10 9 8 7 6 5 4 3 2

ISBN: 978-1-959770-37-4

Cover and interior design: Gary Lindberg

All Oxherding images used with the permission of
Dharma Communications, Inc..

DANCE OF LIGHT

Christian, Sufi and Zen wisdom
for today's spiritual seeker

Alice McDowell, Ph.D.

Wisdom
Editions

Minneapolis, Minnesota

With love and gratitude for my two sons, Aaron and Sean,
and their wonderful families.

Table of Contents

Foreword

by Kyriacos Markides, Ph.D.

From the earliest times, people have looked for meaning in their lives. The famous psychologist, C.G. Jung, claimed part of the human psyche has a spiritual function that actually seeks meaning in life. People are psychologically healthier if they can find significance to life's events, even if they are ultimately untrue. This search for meaning often ignites during times of adversity, whether personal or collective, with the simple question, "Why?" Why is this happening to me at this time? Why is this happening to the world at this time? Somehow humans need to understand the reasons for challenges and hardships. Once found, they can relax—at least marginally. It's somehow easier to accept difficulties in life if there's a purpose to it.

What is the goal of this search for meaning? What do humans really want? The Hindu tradition claims that all humans desire the same ultimate outcome. They want to be alive, to grow in understanding and experience, and to be happy. The Hindu term for this goal is *sat-chit-ananda:* infinite being (existence), infinite awareness (wisdom) and infinite bliss (joy).

The mystics of the world are the experts on how to obtain this goal because they have reached it themselves through their own personal experience. They have found infinite being, awareness and bliss, although many call it by a different name and describe different ways to reach it. In both their own writings and those of their devotees, they have illuminated the way for humanity to follow. Some of these precious writings have fallen into disuse, are difficult to decipher due to their arcane language, or only appear in one tradition.

The work of Alice McDowell expertly retrieves and updates the wisdom of mystics from different traditions as a way to guide aspirants today. Her latest book, *Dance of Light: Christian, Sufi, and Zen Wisdom for Today's Spiritual Seekers,* has the hallmarks of a classic, a labor of love written by a scholar of religion and psychology who is also a spiritual seeker, guide and master. Dr. McDowell combines her stellar academic qualifications with direct and first-hand experiential knowledge of the mystical core of the world's religions in both East and West. She is trained in these mystical pathways through sustained apprenticeships in a great number and variety of retreats with leading Christian contemplatives, Sufis, Buddhist teachers and Zen masters, as well as with celebrated pioneers in transpersonal and humanistic psychology. With such admirable and impressive credentials, Dr. McDowell is the spiritual guide par excellence for a modern age that is open, among other things, to the needs and roles of women in the pursuit of truth and spiritual self-actualization. A globalized and pluralizing world needs spiritual guides who can embrace diversity based on the realization that there must be many paths to the top of the mountain where all cultural differences take a back seat and pure awareness of Divinity resides.

Dr. McDowell's work is beautifully written and free of jargon, thus making it easily accessible to the discerning spiritual seeker. The style of her prose is pollinated with anecdotes and stories from her vast personal repertoire of experiences rendering her book a refreshingly real page turner. Like all spiritual teachers of the great religious traditions, and of the core teaching of transpersonal psychology, she takes for granted the fact that there are clearly discernible stages in the development of consciousness. These are stages which lie beyond the ordinary state of consciousness, within which, alas, academic psychology and positivistic science are currently stranded. In great and lucid detail, she maps the territory of the spiritual journey that lies beyond everyday consciousness and guides the spiritual seeker by pointing out both the glories of the journey inwards and its potential pitfalls. Most importantly, she lays out methods and practices for the seeker to access them, as one moves toward the ultimate goal of knowing oneself and attaining unity consciousness and divine realization. She shows us detailed ways and methodologies on how to overcome spiritual obstacles through the process of purifying our hearts and minds from our addictions and ego attachments that stultify and distort our lives and prevent us from experiencing the divine light. She also offers invaluable advice to the struggling soul on how to effectively navigate through the proverbial and unavoidable "Dark Night of the Soul" as the seeker ascends the pathways upward toward the top of the mountain.

In conclusion, Dr. McDowell's work is a compassionate and brilliant handbook that shows us step by step how to live a spiritual and meaningful life in the modern world and how to discover the divine within, which is our true nature, real homeland and ultimate destination.

Preface

I am uncertain when my spiritual journey began. Maybe all children sense a presence beyond everyday reality as it did for me. I know that at eleven, when my father died, I was desperately seeking answers to larger questions. I felt unsatisfied by my classmates' talk of clothes and boys. I started to attend daily Mass and found solace in the peace it gave me. Much to the chagrin of my high school teachers and classmates headed for Ivy League schools, I decided to go to a Catholic college to find answers to my questions.

College life answered some of my queries, but I continued my search by attending graduate school in religious studies. As my spiritual life was developing, I wanted to know the lay of the land so I wouldn't flounder in the dark, travel down dead-end paths or fall into traps. I needed to know I was traveling in the right direction. I longed for some words of inspiration to stay committed to my spiritual unfoldment. I looked for repeating patterns or the particular ways individuals develop spiritually, hoping to find guidance for my own experiences. I became fascinated with Evelyn Underhill's comprehensive study of the stages of the spiritual journey in her classic book, *Mysticism,* first published in 1911.[1] I found these five stages, based on the writings of Christian mystics from earliest times through the early twentieth century, to be a great guide for understanding the dynamics of the spiritual path and the types of experiences a seeker may encounter.

Later, when I began teaching mysticism at Ithaca College, I found Underhill's outmoded and terse writing too difficult for my students to fully comprehend. As a result, I extracted and updated the buried wisdom in her classical work in my lectures. When I created a new course in world religions, I delighted at the connections between the Christian stages of spiritual journey and other spiritual traditions. The Zen Oxherding pictures—a series of drawings with commentary from the twelfth century—describe the ten steps to enlightenment[2] and remarkably parallel Underhill's schema and other such maps I've researched.

These tools and guidelines prepared me to move deeper into my spiritual life. In 1985, I became an initiate in the Inayati Sufi Order founded by Hazrat Inayat Khan (1882-1927), hereafter referred to as HIK, a path dedicated to deepening the spiritual life regardless of faith, belief or non-belief. More recently, I've studied with Adyashanti, a contemporary American spiritual teacher, who trained in the Zen tradition.

Knowing that my spiritual growth seemed to accelerate during retreats, and wanting others to benefit from this profound process, my husband and I co-founded Light on the Hill Retreat Center, which officially opened in 1991. Light on the Hill gave me a wonderful place to guide others. I love the deep connection that takes place between guide and seeker when both are transformed during the retreat process. In 1998, I founded the Hidden Treasure Program, which focuses on healing deep-seated wounds that block spiritual growth.

After decades of teaching, guiding others, and continuing my own spiritual growth, I awoke one morning to an inner voice. "Write down the wisdom you've gained over the years." *Dance of Light* is my heartfelt response to this sacred directive. I revisited the earlier part of my life when I discovered Evelyn Underhill's stages of the spiritual journey and their similarity to the Zen Oxherding pictures, deciding these would form the pillars of this book.

My knowledge and experience are too limited to compare all the mystical teachings of the different religious traditions. Over the years I have contemplated and loved many of these teachings, which inspire and accompany me in life. Nevertheless, I can only write about what I've studied and experienced, namely Christianity, Sufism and Zen Buddhism through the Oxherding pictures and Adyashanti's teaching.

The insights revealed in *Dance of Light* primarily come from my interplay with these wellsprings of wisdom. Nevertheless, they resonate with the insights found in many other traditions. I believe they will add to the broader conversation about the spiritual life and serve as a guide to your spiritual unfoldment.

May the rich wisdom gleaned from the mystics of different traditions and my dance with them serve as a revealing light to you and other spiritual seekers on this awesome journey.

Chapter 1:
Overview of the Spiritual Path

Do you remember when you began your spiritual odyssey? For some of you, it may have been a sudden event that propelled you to start asking deeper questions: What is the purpose of my life? Is there something more to my life than I'm now experiencing? Are there dimensions of reality beyond my knowledge? Or maybe you sensed a presence or greater reality in your childhood, whether you were born feeling this way or experienced something that brought you a new awareness. Perhaps you were intrigued by spirituality but refrained from considering it part of your life because you didn't have time, you were turned off by hypocritical people, or you were afraid of going down an unknown direction with an unknown outcome.

Going in an uncharted direction to an unknown place *is* scary, but it is also exciting. Do you remember how you felt before you attended school for the first time, started an important job, or got married? Perhaps you were more excited than scared, but the uncertainty about a successful outcome most likely loomed somewhere in your psyche. Similarly, you may also feel scared and excited when deciding to venture more deeply into your spiritual life.

Perhaps you already follow a spiritual path but have reached a point of "unknowing" that confounds you. Whether a novice or seasoned seeker, you might be wondering: Will I get lost in this uncharted territory? Will I mistakenly travel down a dead-end path and be disappointed? Will I be overwhelmed and not make progress? Will I become some kind of spiritual fanatic or lose touch with reality?

You may have arrived at a place where something inside you says there's no other option but to move forward. But how? At this point, you might seek some kind of guidance. Perhaps you've already read books, attended online teachings or worked with a spiritual teacher to find answers but sense you need something more. This book is intended for you wherever you are on your spiritual path.

From the earliest times, the world's great wisdom traditions have outlined the stages of the journey as a guide for the spiritual seeker. *Dance of Light* interprets and expands this guidance with particular focus on the stages outlined in Evelyn Underhill's *Mysticism*[3] and the Zen Oxherding pictures[4]. The Sufis also speak of developmental stages for spiritual growth, which are called stations (*malqamat*).[5]

This book elucidates the kinds of experiences you may encounter on your way toward wholeness and puts them in a cross-cultural and interfaith framework. It will guide you through your spiritual unfoldment, provide you with a light into the unknown, steer you away from its pitfalls and inspire you with its joyful possibilities. Interspersed throughout the book are stories from my own life journey and from Christian, Sufi, Zen and other traditions—some humorous, some thought-provoking, some poetic—all aimed at giving you further insight into your spiritual life. Topics for further reflection or practices appear at the end of each chapter. These encourage you to deepen your own experience during the journey.

Ultimately, you will cross the unknown desert alone. Guides and teachings can serve as midwives, but you are the one having the baby.

Comparing Eastern and Western Traditions

Until recently, most books on the spiritual life focused on a particular religious tradition or an individual's personal experience. *Dance of Light* looks at the spiritual life through the mystical teachings of many spiritual traditions. This approach reveals similarities between these traditions that aren't apparent when focusing on their doctrines and rituals. Recognizing the common ground at the heart of all religious traditions helps heal the divisions between them—divisions that have created wars, intolerance and hatred. If you think of the spiritual journey as a mountain to be climbed, the doctrines and rituals of the various traditions are like encampments around its base. They appear far apart and look quite different from each other. As you climb higher, they seem to grow closer.

If you have found your home in the tradition of your birth, *Dance of Light* will help you dive deeper into it and enrich your belief. In addition to fostering more tolerance, learning about the similarities between faiths helps you to better understand your own. I experienced a deeper understanding of the rosary when I discovered how prayers with beads were a common practice in Buddhism, Hinduism and Sufism. I realized there was something about the movement of the fingers along the beads that grounded the prayers and affected the whole body.

Perhaps, however, you have been turned off by some of the superficial and hard-to-believe teachings of Western religions. You may have turned to Eastern spiritualities to satisfy the deep longing in your heart, not realizing the similarities between these teachings and Western mystical tradition.[6] Maybe, you've erroneously compared the religious views and customs of the West, such as the overseeing of woman's productive rights, with the mystical writings of the East.

During graduate school, I recall how excited my student friends and I felt about attending a party during which we shared insights into Buddhism. But one of our classmates, a student from Taiwan, vehemently opposed attending. Surprised by her response, I asked her why. She told me that to her, Buddhism meant her mother bargaining in the temple for her sister's marriage, and she would have none of it. Aha, I thought, so Buddhism has their own questionable beliefs and practices annexed to their authentic teachings just like Western traditions do. *Dance of Light* endeavors to eliminate these false comparisons by correlating the authentic teachings of each tradition.

The Direct and Indirect Paths

Some spiritual teachings advocate jumping into the unknown without much instruction so you don't get stuck in an intellectual understanding of the journey or get distracted by the practices, methodologies and intermediate stages. This is the direct path. Many wonderful teachers today offer this path as a way to spiritual realization. If you have the courage to delve into the unknown by being present to each moment, concentrating on emptiness, or by asking a repeating question—such as, Who or what am I?—the direct path may be appropriate for you. It bypasses the risk of measuring your spiritual progress by preconceived ideas that might not be what's true or best for you in the moment. It also prevents you from falling into the trap of thinking you *should* follow these ideas all the time. The direct path allows you to evolve in your own way.

But there are dangers in the direct path as well. It may make it difficult to integrate your realization into your daily life. A sudden awakening experience, which most often stems from this approach, may cause you to become disoriented. You could find yourself confused or overwhelmed as your relationships, profession or self-identity no longer make sense.

The direct path also circumvents the intermediate levels of reality, which are included in the indirect path. These encompass the realm of creative imagination—the inspirational source of poetry, music and the arts—the angelic domain of purity and beauty, the universal forms or building blocks of the universe, and spheres of dazzling light, all of which lend richness to the journey. If you follow the direct path, you may find yourself in one of these realms but feel disoriented since you haven't learned about them.

Following the indirect path, however, also has its dangers. You may become distracted by its richness, intricate practices and variety of experiences. You may even get stuck at one of the intermediate levels of consciousness and be unable to proceed.

Many spiritual traditions include both paths. In Christianity, the direct path is called apophatic mysticism or *via negativa*. Here, the seeker negates any positive descriptions of the Divine and all the intermediate stages of the journey to beeline for the ultimate goal. John of the Cross (1542–1591), who speaks of traveling to the Divine in darkness and by night[7], and Meister Eckhart (c1260–c1328), who claimed that God cannot be described with any words, images or concepts[8], are great examples of this path.

The indirect path, called kataphatic mysticism or *via positiva*, includes positive descriptions of the Radiant All, such as light, life and love. It accepts everything—nature, everyday reality, the intermediate realms, and experiencing the Divine as Other—before reaching the final goal. Exemplifying the indirect path are St. Francis (1182–1226), who loved nature[9]; the priest-paleontologist, Teilhard de Chardin (1881–1955), who speaks of the spiritual power of matter[10]; and the abbess and visionary Hildegard of Bingen (1098-1179), who composed beautiful music still heard today, wrote a scientific text, and engaged in political action[11].

Unlike today's emphasis on the mindfulness and nonduality of the direct path, some contemporary writers spotlight the indirect path. In *Wild Mercy*[12], Mirabai Starr demonstrates how the feminine journey includes embracing the body and all of life's experiences for spiritual realization. In her most recent book, *Eye of the Heart*[13], Cynthia Bourgeault reestablishes and focuses on the intermediate realms of reality and how they interact with our everyday life.

In addition to one tradition including both paths, a single person may toggle back and forth between them. Paul Brunton claims this is the best way to proceed. "The wiser and philosophical procedure is to coupe together the work on both paths in a regular alternative rhythm, so that during the course of a year or two totally different kinds of result begin to appear in the character and behaviour [sic], in the consciousness and understanding."[14] Beverly Lanzetta in *The Monk Within* introduces the term *via feminina*[15], which includes the solitude and silence of the monastic life with social reform. To my mind, this way belongs to both paths.

Whether you follow the direct or indirect path or alternate between them, you ultimately end up in the same or similar place of complete spiritual realization or union with all reality—your true home. You have simply followed one of several different routes.

Stages of the Journey

I didn't know about the direct path when I started my spiritual odyssey. Instead, I was somehow guided toward a gentler, longer and indirect path that offers the benefits of diverse practices and outlines steps and stages along the way. *Dance of Light* focuses on the full trajectory of this indirect path, taking you from a place of unknowing, to your first inkling that there is something more than everyday consciousness, to finding a path that will take you there. At some place in the journey, you may experience the awakening stage, a radical experience which takes you out of your usual perceptions and ushers in a new, greater understanding of reality.

A large part of the spiritual journey involves the purification or self-simplification stage—a releasing of all that no longer aligns with your True Nature. The journey continues through the illumination stage of dazzling light, the dark night of the soul, and finally to a permanent realization of your True Nature, called "enlightenment" or "spiritual realization" in some traditions and "union with the Divine" in others. Although *Dance of Light* delineates these stages in a logical order for the purpose of clarity, you may experience them in any order, oscillating back and forth between them.

Some claim that this traditional model of the stages of the journey to a place beyond this world is a masculine (not necessarily male) model, having mostly been created and articulated by men throughout the centuries. Nevertheless, this way has spoken to me and many other women throughout history. Diamonds of truth can certainly be extracted from this traditional model for everyone's benefit. *Dance of Light* adds feminist voices in conjunction with the Sufi mysticism of Hazrat Inayat Khan. In many ways, this teaching advocates a feminine viewpoint with its emphasis on growth through the natural world, a goal of living a harmonious life in *this* world, and purification through love.[16]

Awareness of the stages outlined in *Dance of Light* is most helpful if taken as a guide that may need to be disregarded at times. This prevents you from taking the insights presented here as absolute truth and allows the unfolding of your spiritual life in its own organic way. However, knowing about the trajectory of the path can orient you in the right direction and support your journey. If you find you're dwelling in a place of unknowing, you need not despair but can take comfort from understanding that this is an acknowledged part of the journey. If you aggrandize your spiritual experiences or regret your lack of them, you can learn that there are more important aspects to the path.

Sometimes the spiritual way feels like traveling in an airplane through the clouds to a place you've never been before. It's difficult to orient yourself because you can't see the sky above or the earth below. During this experience, you know you are moving, and you have a vague understanding of the destination, but that's about all. You only hope the pilot knows how to reach your destination. It takes courage to trust the pilot and venture into the unknown.

In truth, not-knowing can be a good companion on the path. It helps you surrender to a greater knowing. If you practice a spiritual discipline, attend retreats or read spiritual books, you sense you are moving forward even though you don't know what the end point will be. If you don't have a practice, you are still moving anyway. I love what the Sufi master, Hazrat Inayat Khan, says about this.

> Everyone, whether conscious or unconscious, is striving towards spiritual attainment—happiness, peace, knowledge, aliveness, power. The only difference is that one who is attracted by it faces one's goal, making his way towards it, while the other has his back on it and is drawn towards the goal without being conscious of it. Poor person, he does not know where he is being taken, but he goes just the same; his punishment is that he does not see the glory he is approaching, and his torture is that he is being drawn towards the opposite pole to that which he desires.[17]

Journey or No Journey?

Some spiritual teachings claim you are already enlightened, so why speak about a journey? As Ekai Kawaguchi (1866–1945) in *The Gateless Gate* claims:

> Before the first step is taken the goal is reached.
> Before the tongue is moved the speech is finished.
> More than brilliant intuition is needed
> To find the origin of the right road.[18]

When I first heard this teaching, I couldn't accept it. I didn't feel "enlightened." How could that be possible? I am now able to say, "Yes, it's right here—beingness, aliveness, love—they are right here." This formlessness is in—and beyond—all things. It is the greater me and the greater you. How did I get from my first reaction to my present realization? That's the journey! It entails moving from not seeing to seeing what is actually always here.

In other words, the journey is moving from your ego consciousness, which doesn't feel enlightened, to the consciousness of your radiant True Nature. It involves allowing the many obstacles that block higher consciousness to surface and be transformed. The ups and downs of the journey is a laborious one, requiring discipline and surrender. For me, it has taken decades of life experiences, challenges and retreats to get to a place of open but still intermittent awareness—and I know I still have more traveling to do.

Goal of the Journey

What is the goal of the spiritual journey? For most traditions, the goal is two-fold: realization of Supreme Reality, whether you experience it as within or beyond you, and expressing that realization in everyday life. Adyashanti describes this two-fold process as always being and always becoming.

Different traditions use different words to refer to goal of the journey—enlightenment, True Nature, God consciousness, Ultimate Reality, final awakening or simply love. I like using the terms "Radiant All" or "Great Mystery," even though the nature of this Supreme Reality is beyond words. Although these concepts are not necessarily equivalent, they convey the same core sense of an eternal reality.

The second facet of the goal is radiating the Great Mystery in your own unique way as you become a compassionate and healing presence in the world. This is a dynamic, ever-growing process. Adyashanti claims the purpose of life is "to be free and to love in such a way that your presence redeems the sorrow of life."[19] A particular spiritual tradition may emphasize one of these facets over the other, but both constitute the awakening process.[20]

Your understanding of the Great Mystery won't come from the descriptions of others. It will arise through your own experience. The wisdom teachers have pointed the way through their words and, better yet, through their embodiment of the teachings. Your own core experience will always be the best guide.

On reaching final realization many find it is not what they imagined it to be. You may think it will bring an end to suffering, but you are sure to be disappointed. You might erroneously think you're supposed to become like Buddha, Jesus or some other self-realized being, when the goal is to become a unique expression of your widening awareness of the true nature of reality. Rabbi Susya said: "In the world to come, I will not be asked why I was not Moses, I will be asked why I was not Susya."[21] The Bhagavad Gita says: "And do thy duty (life's purpose), even if it be humble, rather than another's, even if it be great. To die in one's duty is life: to live in another's is death."[22] In other words, you're asked to simply be your true self.

Hazrat Inayat Khan (hereafter HIK) dismisses the false expectations followers may have of the Sufi path such as developing psychic powers, studying spiritual texts, giving up worldly pursuits or spending long periods of time in seclusion. He claims the object of the path "is to become human, to find the way how to become human, how to live a human being's life to its fullness, how to live a life of love, harmony and beauty."[23] I'm sure you've discovered that it's not an easy task to live a life of love, harmony and beauty. Sudden eruptions of anger, fear and blame block your desire for harmony. Not getting your way, feeling abandoned, or becoming stuck in your life are other blocks to living a loving and harmonious life.

Dance of Light offers wisdom gleaned from the great mystics ranging from earliest times to the present day along with guidelines on how to clear these blocks so you can live a life of love, harmony and beauty. May their insights inspire and encourage you to dedicate yourself to this awesome path.

Chapter 2:
Dappled Light–The Dark Wood

Midway in our life's journey, I went astray
From the straight road and woke to find myself
Alone in a dark wood.[24]

–Dante, *The Divine Comedy*, first canto

The spiritual journey can begin with—and periodically return to—a place of not knowing who you are or why you're here. Have you ever felt this way? You thought you knew where you were going and suddenly something changed. You may have experienced the death of a loved one, a serious illness, a divorce or burn-out in your career. In this place of uncertainty, you may no longer have the energy to do what you've always been doing in your life. Inwardly, everything comes to a stop, while outwardly you may go through the motions. It's like falling through space—a most uncomfortable and even scary place. You might ask: Who am I? What is the purpose of my life anyway? Nothing feels right.

If you've been consciously traveling the spiritual path for some time, the Dark Wood Stage can occur when your old practices no longer have the same effect. Your old understanding of spirituality or the Divine no longer fits.

Holy Saturday: A Place of Not Knowing

In the Christian tradition, the Dark Wood Stage is likened to Holy Saturday—the day between the crucifixion on Good Friday and the resurrection on Easter Sunday. It was a desert time when Jesus' followers felt bereft and their beliefs about Jesus had been shattered. Even though nothing was visibly happening on Holy Saturday, tradition claims that during this time Jesus went into the underworld to liberate souls stuck in limbo and waiting to enter heaven. In your personal life, it might appear that nothing happens during the Dark Wood Stage of your journey, but during that stage you are preparing for the next stage of your journey. That preparation occurs at an unconscious level.

I experienced the Dark Wood Stage for over a year after the publication of my book, *Hidden Treasure,* and the releasing of my administrative duties at Light on the Hill. I tried writing, but nothing inspired me. I read mysteries, worked on puzzles and watched movies. I continued teaching the Hidden Treasure course and guiding retreats, but I experienced an emptiness inside. It felt like I was falling through space with no sense that I would ever land. This is a different kind of emptiness than experienced near the end of the journey, which paradoxically brings a feeling of completeness and fullness.

Most likely, you'll encounter the Dark Wood Stage more than once. It's called growth. Whether conscious or not, you've completed a certain cycle and are waiting for the next step to appear.

First Oxherding Picture:
Seeking the Ox (Buddha Nature)

The first Oxherding picture, *Seeking the Ox,* describes the Dark Wood Stage this way:

> Desolate through forests and fearful in jungles,
> he is seeking an Ox which he does not find.
> Up and down dark, nameless, wide-flowing rivers,
> in deep mountain thickets he treads many bypaths.
> Bone-tired, heart-weary, he carries on his search
> for this something which he yet cannot find.
> At evening he hears cicadas chirping in the trees.[25]

As this Oxherding picture portrays, instead of bewilderment, your Dark Wood might be a time of frantic but futile outward searching. In truth, it's better to move inward, into the depths of your own being. This is an excellent time for going on retreat. It can be comforting to know that you are not going crazy but are experiencing an important stage in the journey. Rushing through it often leads to further problems down the road.

The commentary on this first Zen Oxherding picture states: "The Ox has never really gone astray so why search for it? Having turned his back on his True-nature, the man cannot see it. Because of his defilements he has lost sight of the Ox."[26]

"The Ox has never gone astray" implies that you are already enlightened. Although true, you might find such a claim frustrating, as I did. You might think, *I don't feel enlightened.* Of course, you may have the wrong idea of what enlightenment is. You may think it means all struggles will disappear or you'll walk around in a state of bliss. Even if you have a deeper and more refined understanding of enlightenment, you may still feel frustrated because you know you haven't consciously reached it. The writer of the commentary on the first Oxherding picture tells us why. Your defilement—or the blocks arising from psychological and emotional wounds, programming, distractions or addictions—prevents you from seeing what is already there.

Compare the Dark Wood experience to climbing a ladder. When your foot leaves one rung, it hangs in the air briefly before arriving at the next one. This is also true for the spiritual journey. When the Dark Wood surfaces in your life, it simply means you are leaving the old behind and are left hanging while waiting for the new to arrive. You are actually making spiritual progress, even though it doesn't feel that way.

Temptation to Return to the Old or Find an Unsuitable New

Two dangers can occur during the Dark Wood Stage. You might be tempted to go back to the old way of being and doing, to what is comfortable and familiar. You might say, "Maybe, if I work harder, I'll regain fulfillment in my career or relationship. At least it was safe. I wouldn't feel so bereft."

Many who take this route become discouraged or depressed down the road. Going back to your old way of being usually does not work. The Dark Wood tells you that your past has died, and you need to move on.

The other danger is pushing too quickly to find something new—a new relationship, job, spiritual practice or teacher—only to discover later it was the wrong choice. The relationship or job doesn't bring the fulfillment you expected. Desperation at the onset is a sign that it probably will not work out well. As hard as it may be, if you stay in this uncomfortable place of unknowing, you will eventually experience a notion of how to proceed. This produces more lasting results. That inner stirring might appear as a sudden knowing of the next step, or it may come as an idea suggested by someone else or an outside circumstance that evokes an inner yes.

Many describe the Dark Wood as a most promising stage because it's a place of pure potentiality. Any possibility might pop up at any time. It's similar to the concept of "beginner's mind" in the Zen tradition, a time when you're open to the new without carrying baggage from the past. It's a place where you can experience the Divine within—if you stay with it long enough. Knowing that the Dark Wood is a recognized stage on the spiritual path and not some weird aberration may not take away the scariness or feeling of dissolution, but it can make it easier to endure. You are making spiritual progress!

Reflections on the Dark Wood

When in the Dark Wood stage:

1. You could continue with your spiritual practices, even though they may feel dry and unappealing. Maintaining your practices shows a commitment to your spiritual path—a commitment that goes beyond the need for some kind of consolation or spiritual experience.

2. You could be aware of any impulses you may feel to return to the old ways or rush into something new.

3. It might help to ponder the saying by Jesse Lair, "I don't know where I'm going, but I sure ain't lost."[27] If you keep looking ahead to see what's next, you won't be paying attention to where you are in the moment and may miss your footing.

4. You could become more aware of the emptiness you feel and keep concentrating on the feelings that arise, observing how they change. In most cases, such a practice will eventually change scary feelings into peaceful ones. This alleviates your anxiety about being in this state.

5. You may want to look over your life and recall times when you've previously landed in this place. How successfully did you navigate it? Was it difficult for you to be comfortable here? Did you act too quickly, going back to the old or rushing into something new? What was the outcome? Do you now see what needed to fall away and what took its place? Can you see the trajectory of your path more clearly?

Chapter 3:
A Light on Your Path–Finding the Way

Fortunately, the Dark Wood Stage is temporary. How long it lasts varies with each person and each situation. If you haven't succumbed to the dangers of the Dark Wood—going back to the old or rushing too quickly into the new—your next step will be revealed. Deep inside, you'll feel the rightness of the way forward. This can take many different forms—a new job or creative venture, a new relationship, an inspiring person or spiritual teacher, a meditative practice, an insightful book, journaling or some inner shift that somehow moves you forward. In the middle of his own Dark Wood, Dante found Virgil, who would serve as his guide for the first part of his journey. Finding the Way is a more heartening stage than the Dark Wood because you realize there *is* a path—a way out of this place of disorientation and unknowing.

Second Oxherding Picture:
Finding the Tracks

The second Zen Oxherding picture, titled *Finding the Tracks*, also points to a way out of the Dark Wood. In this case, the tracks are Buddhist scriptures and teachings. "Through the sutras and teachings he discerns the tracks of the Ox. He has not actually entered the gate, but he sees in a tentative way the tracks of the Ox."[28]

Finding the Tracks tells you the Ox (your Buddha nature) is real! Something is making those tracks. Your search has not been in vain. After the initial elation of finding the tracks, you may become impatient, wanting to experience more than just the tracks. Yes, you most likely find the peace and centeredness of meditation lovely, but you may desire more. You might wonder, How do I connect with my own True Nature? or How can I become enlightened as soon as possible? Eventually, you may question whether the path you've chosen is the right one. Zen teachers advise to keep meditating. Daily meditation practice and letting go of preconceived ideas shows you the way.

If you have been traveling the spiritual path for some time, the Finding the Way stage may entail discovering a new, more relevant practice or way to engage in your present practice. You may decide after inner reflection to work with a new teacher or a new set of teachings. You may desire—and be presented with—a job more aligned with your inner life. You may simply have more clarity in your life or find your intuition more developed.

The Dark Wood Stage does not necessarily precede the Finding the Way Stage. As you recall, the stages are not in any particular order and individuals dance between them in their own unique ways. My experiences of finding inspiring people and a guide came before encountering the Dark Wood. This oscillation between the Dark Wood and Finding the Way may happen many times throughout your journey.

Inspiring People Who Point the Way

Encountering inspiring people can show you a way out of the Dark Wood or galvanize you to begin or continue the spiritual journey. Inspiring people may motivate you to embody their qualities. During my time in graduate school, I met several inspiring teachers. One such teacher, Fr. George Maloney,[29] was a Jesuit priest of the Russian Byzantine Rite and my mysticism professor. He struck me as a person on fire with love. He radiated an intensity for living life to the fullest in all he did. I wanted to be like him.

On one occasion, I met him on a campus pathway with many students swirling around us. I felt like time stood still. With intense eyes, he said, "Alice, how wonderful to meet you! How are your classes going?" I felt he had all the time in the world for me and that I was the only person in his life. And, at that moment, I was. Something magical happened during that simple exchange because I can still see him standing there and talking to me as vividly as when we actually met.

I also had the good fortune to study with Fr. Thomas Berry[30], a pioneer in the field of ecology and spirituality. He possessed a deep sympathy for all of life, which he poetically expressed. He opened me to the value of all religious traditions. In referring to other religions, he would say: "I don't just want roses in my garden, I want tulips, daffodils and all kinds of flowers." He also said, "There should be a world Bible with the sacred scriptures from all the religious traditions contained within."

> **Would You Think It Odd?**
>
> Would you think it odd if Hafiz said,
>
> "I am in love with every church
> And mosque
> And temple
> And any kind of shrine
>
> Because I know it is there
> That people say the different names
> Of the One God."
>
> –Hafiz, *I Heard God Laughing*[31]

Sometimes, inspiration from a person requires no words at all. At a conference on spirituality at St. John the Divine in New York City, an announcement came over the speaker that Swami Satchidananda would lead a class on yoga. At the start of the class, when the Swami stood up in that beautiful sanctuary filled with attentive listeners and surrounded by stained glass windows, I became immediately struck by the magnetism of his whole being. His eyes were aglow and his stance majestic. I thought, "He knows something I don't know, and I want to know it!"

Finding and Working with a Spiritual Guide

Being inspired by someone and actually working with a spiritual guide are two very different experiences. In the latter case, the bond between the seeker and guide grows deeper and more intimate. Usually, you have an inner knowing or a significant outer sign confirming that this person is to be your mentor. Some people have dreams of their guides before meeting them. Others come to a quiet, inner realization that this particular person is to be their spiritual director. Still others have dramatic first encounters with their guide.

Just after graduate school, I became acquainted with a priest who radiated a wonderful peace and depth. Before he had become a priest, he'd spent a year in solitude during which he had deeply experienced the workings of the inner life. Previously, I had never thought of asking someone to be my guide, but something prompted me to ask him. He gave me a small book called *The Radiant Heart*[32] to see if I resonated with it. The book was written by Linda Sabbath, one of the founders of the Thomas Merton Center for Contemplative Prayer, where Fr. John had spent six of his twelve months on retreat.

The founders of this center had traveled all over the world to discover spiritual practices in the Eastern traditions only to find similar practices in Christian mystical writings. I saw that the foreword was written by my mysticism professor, Fr. George Maloney. The book's approach of seeing similarities in the world religions reminded me of Fr. Thomas Berry, another inspiring teacher. Its title, *The Radiant Heart*, pointed to my own heart-centered spiritual path. These signs and my own inner confirmation indicated that Fr. John was to be my guide, the first of several on my journey.

My significant yet humble discovery of Fr. John contrasts with Paramahansa Yogananda's more dramatic and heart-felt meeting with his guide, Sri Yukteswar. After continually pleading for a guide, Yogananda one day heard a voice saying he would meet his guide that very day. On a shopping errand, he saw what he described as "a Christlike man in ocher robes motionless at the end of a lane."[33] This man seemed familiar, but Yogananda walked on. The farther away he walked, the more leaden his feet became. When Yogananda turned around, the feeling in his feet became normal. After wavering back and forth several times, Yogananda realized that this holy man had been magnetically attracting him. He raced back to find him. Kneeling at his feet in humility, he now realized he had seen the image of this man in numerous dreams and visions. I love Yukteswar's response: "O my own, you have come to me! How many years I have waited for you!"[34]

Although the particulars of working with a spiritual guide may vary, most guides know the inner workings of your spiritual life, encourage you to move beyond your ego limitations, and help prevent you from traveling down unproductive paths. Sitting in a rectory room during one of my spiritual direction sessions with Fr. John, I was taken aback when he responded to something I said.

"Look at all the I's, me's and mine's in what you just said." In one sentence, he sliced through my egoic way of thinking. Another time, he admonished me: "You are too attached to the future." This caused me to ask myself important questions: What is the right relationship to my future? How can I stay more in the present moment?

The guide evaluates events in your life as learning opportunities for spiritual development. I remember that Fr. John got excited when I told him I had allowed my department head to determine my teaching schedule. This seemed like such a trivial matter to me, but to him it exemplified surrendering my ego desires—an important and necessary part of the path. In the same session, he barely reacted when I told him about a deep spiritual experience. His action gently conveyed the inessential need to focus on spiritual experiences.

Without speaking a word, a guide can be a catalyst for deep insight, opening you to what lies beyond everyday reality. Students of HIK would prepare certain questions to ask him during an upcoming private interview and then find themselves so overcome by his radiant presence that they forgot their questions. To their surprise, they realized they had learned their answers after leaving. One time, while on a retreat, I struggled to figure out the meaning of a dream when suddenly it became clear. I looked up to find that Pir Vilayat Khan had just walked into the room. These examples show how a guide's simple presence can bring needed insight to your spiritual life.

The role of the guide is similar to that of a midwife who nudges, cajoles, encourages and supports the birthing process. Nevertheless, it is the mother, not she, who is having the baby. Similarly, the guide oversees and encourages you, but you are the one integrating the insights and undergoing the transformation. You alone are the one who needs to become conscious of your True Nature.

Another role of the guide is to become obsolete. This means the guide helps you connect with your true inner guidance, so you no longer depend on an outer guide for navigating your life. As a result of life's challenges or some inherent gift, some individuals develop inner guidance without an outer guide. However, in this case, the danger for self-deception is much greater. These individuals may think they're making progress or are on the right track when they are not.

Group Guidance

Interest in spirituality has spawned several forms of group guidance. Many of today's spiritual teachers have become so popular that it would be impossible for their students to form a one-to-one relationship with them. Adyashanti uses the group model. To receive guidance in this form, students read his books, attend one of his retreats, do a virtual retreat or listen to his weekly broadcasts during which a few are able to ask questions. Even if you don't personally ask a question during a retreat or broadcast, you might receive the answers you need through a response to someone else's question. You may also receive guidance internally, especially when attending retreats and physically being in his presence. If you still think you need more personal direction, Adyashanti's assistants are available to help. At other times, you can call his headquarters and speak to a counselor. This model works well for large groups of seekers.

With our limited view of how guidance works, you might think group guidance wouldn't work as well as the traditional one-to-one model. Having experienced both forms, I think each one is effective in its own way. I've appreciated the personal guidance I received from Fr. John and my Sufi guide, Aziza. I've also been deeply changed from retreats with Adyashanti and leaders of the Inayati Sufi Order.

Recently, I attended a leaders' retreat led by Pir Zia, HIK's grandson and present head of the Inayati Sufi Order. During one early morning practice on the beach, we were to receive a special initiation/blessing. About eighty of us held onto a rope that snaked through our group. I staunchly doubted the efficacy of this method until I felt a strong jolt throughout my whole body and sensed a presence blessing me from a higher realm. This instilled in me the potency of group healing and guidance.

Another form of group guidance occurs when individuals come together to help each other clear obstacles to their spiritual growth. For more than twenty years, I've facilitated such groups in the Hidden Treasure Program and always marveled at how deeply members were able to heal and guide one another. Participants were profoundly touched by their classmates' honesty when describing their life struggles. I noticed how one person's process ignited something in another student that otherwise may never have surfaced. No matter what the format, such authentic sharing opens hearts. The love that pours forth heals and supports others, giving each person confidence to make the changes needed to heal, thus bringing them closer to living a life of love, harmony and beauty.

Conclusion

Finding the Way instinctively feels more secure than the Dark Wood experience. There's a light showing you a path. At the very least, you feel you have a path to follow. You may encounter people who inspire you, begin working with a guide, find a spiritual tradition or teacher that speaks to you or join a group dedicated to personal and spiritual growth. You may start to devote yourself to meditation or other spiritual practices. If you're a seasoned traveler, Finding the Way might take the form of a new or deepening spiritual practice, a sudden insight on how to proceed or perhaps a different teacher or community. It may be years before you actually encounter the Ox, but that's okay. You are learning perseverance and discipline—necessary qualities for navigating the vicissitudes of the spiritual path.

Reflections on Finding the Way

1. If you experienced the Dark Wood state of nothing-is-happening, what signs and experiences led you out of this place? Did someone tell you about a workshop or retreat? Were you drawn to a teacher? Were you excited by a book?

2. If you've found yourself in the Dark Wood more than once, was the way out different each time?

3. Who inspired you to travel the spiritual path? Has your life changed in any way from knowing them? It's heart-opening to remember these precious ones.

4. Do you have a spiritual guide? If not, do you feel called to seek one?

5. Who served as your formal or informal guides over the years? You could take a moment to inwardly thank them for their help in your spiritual growth.

Chapter 4:
Initiating Light-Awakening

As I was watching [the sun] rise, suddenly, in a moment, a veil seemed to be lifted from my eyes. I found the world wrapped in an inexpressible glory with its waves of joy and beauty bursting and breaking on all sides. The thick cloud of sorrow that lay on my heart in many folds was pierced through and through by the light of the world, which was everywhere radiant.

—Tagore[35]

The Awakening Stage is a radical experience that briefly takes you out of your everyday perception of reality and forces you to see it in a new way. It is a shattering event, an initiation. A new world opens up and you see how your previous understanding of the world is only part of a much greater whole. You may have *believed* this greater whole exists, but now you know it in the depths of your being. It's similar to focusing a pair of binoculars until suddenly everything becomes clear, except for one thing—you are not doing the focusing. It happens *to* you, and when things become blurry again, you don't know how to get that focus back. Though brief, this experience changes you forever. You can't deny this greater reality because you know that what you experienced is true. After an awakening experience, you long to have a more lasting or permanent experience of this reality and are willing to undergo the inevitable discipline and trials needed to get there. An awakening experience gives you strength for the journey ahead.

Awakening can happen at any time in your spiritual development. It might occur early and spark your interest in following the spiritual life. It might occur after years of spiritual practice, discipline and life experience.

During this stage, you may experience an awakening so intense that your personal world no longer works. It may be difficult to keep a job or be in a relationship, and you may not even know who you are. If you find yourself in this state, it's helpful to seek out a guide who can help you navigate your difficult and disruptive passage. Fortunately, most do not experience such a radical change in consciousness. Usually, it occurs gradually. Many spiritual experiences might build until there is a quiet shift that totally changes your world view.

Intermittent and Permanent Awakening vs. Spiritual Experiences

In *The End of Your World*, Adyashanti speaks of two kinds of awakening—abiding and non-abiding.[36] The first is permanent, whereas the second is intermittent. A sudden permanent shift is rare. Most likely, if you've had an awakening experience, it's non-abiding. However, even a non-abiding awakening can be a transformative step along the way. Making a distinction between these two kinds of awakenings helps you understand there is more to the journey than you imagined. It encourages you to aim toward the permanent kind.

The Christian tradition uses the term "awakening" to describe a fleeting glimpse of Reality—an infrequent light—and applies the word "illumination" for longer, but still intermittent, awakening—a blinking light. It employs the term "union" for abiding awakening—a steady light. This differs from Adyashanti's broader use of the term, which includes awakening, illumination and union combined.

Adyashanti also distinguishes between abiding or non-abiding awakening and spiritual experiences.[37] Awakening involves a shift in consciousness, a direct experience of the Radiant All which totally changes your world view. It remains at your core even if you can't consciously experience it at all times. Spiritual experiences are often euphoric. You may sense a higher presence, deep peace, expansiveness and new understanding, but eventually you go back to your same world, encouraged by your experiences, perhaps, but not changed at the core of your being. This distinction is important, so don't mistake them thinking you've briefly experienced final realization when in fact you've just had a spiritual experience (wonderful as it may be). Like awakening, spiritual experiences entice you to further spiritual growth and help sustain you during difficult times.

Christian, Sufi and Feminist Awakening Experiences

St. Paul's conversion experience (Acts 9:3-4 and 7-9)[38] is an example of awakening. Previously, he persecuted the budding communities dedicated to Jesus' teachings. One day, when he was traveling to Damascus, he suddenly experienced a heavenly light around him. "He fell to the ground and heard a voice saying, 'Saul, Saul, why are you persecuting me?'" Corroborating his encounter, those traveling with him could also hear the voice but couldn't see anyone. Saul's awakening experience was so profound that he became blind and could not eat or drink for three days. His world turned upside down. He changed his name and saw reality in a new way. Instead of oppressing Christianity, he now became one of its greatest proponents.

Pir Vilayat Khan (1916–2004), in *Call of the Dervish,* gives a more modern account of his awakening. He was told by fellow seekers to go to India and find a dervish who would awaken him. Once in India and after encountering many frustrations in his search for such a dervish, he suddenly encountered him:

> All of a sudden that being is in front of you, and you just don't believe it. He looks more far-out than you could possibly imagine. He's dressed in an old mattress and has ten rings on each hand. He's got eyes of fire, and he looks at you and says, "You there." You're completely nonplussed—you can't think what to say. . . . You try to recover from the shock and follow him, but by that time he's lost in a crowd. Then you realize that you came to India just for that moment when he said, "You there." What did he do at that moment? Somehow, he awakened you,

and you'll never be the same afterwards. That's the way of the dervish: he awakens you.

It's all part of the encounter with something that is so strong that it transforms you, shatters you in your sense of yourself, perplexes you. "Perplexity" is a key word: it's something that you can't fathom—you can't work it out. It's so challenging to your way of thinking that it leaves a mark on you and you can never be the same.[39]

What a beautiful, compelling description of how an awakening experience can shatter your sense of self and your world view just as it did for St. Paul.

Awakening experiences can happen at any age, even to children. The artist, writer and follower of the feminine way, Meinrad Craighead (1936-2019) experienced an awakening at age seven when looking into her dog's eyes.

At this particular moment I was allowed to see infinity through my dog's eyes, and I was old enough to know that. They were as deep, as bewildering, as unattainable as a night sky. Just as mysterious was a clear awareness of water within me, the sound in my ears, yet resounding from my breast. It was a rumbling, rushing sound, the sound of moving water, water-fall water, white water. And I understood that these two things went together—the depth of a dark infinity and this energy of water. I understood "This is who God is." My Mother is water, and she is inside me and I am in the water. . . . And I heard a word—"Come." And that was the beginning of my journey. It was an invitation . . . to be on the journey with this person who spoke to me.[40]

This account contains similar characteristics to St. Paul's and Pir Vilayat Khan's awakenings—a total change in world view and an encounter with another dimension of reality, only it's gentler and begins with a concentration on an element from nature, namely her dog's eyes.

Your experience of awakening may have been initiated by another person, as in Pir Vilayat's encounter, but it could also happen spontaneously, as in St. Paul's and Meinrad Craighead's experiences. My own experience belongs to the spontaneous category. I hesitated to write about it because it's so precious and personal, but I decided to include it because it leads into the following discussion of the three kinds of awakening.

As a college undergrad I attended a two-day silent retreat on campus. Retreats have always been fertile ground for my spiritual journey, but I don't recall anything of significance occurring at this one. Afterward, my friends and I trooped down to the local ice cream parlor, happily chatting because we were no longer required to maintain silence. That evening, when sitting on my dorm room bed, I suddenly felt an intense fire inside and around me. I heard the following words: "My Heart is joined to yours." The memory of this astonishing event has stayed with me my whole life and is as vivid now as when it first occurred decades ago. It opened me to another level of reality.

My understanding of this awakening experience has changed over time. For many years, I thought the words I heard represented a duality. God as other was joined to my separate heart. This changed when I discovered the Sufi concept of the subtle heart, which lies at a deeper, more transpersonal level than the personal heart. Either during meditation, especially when concentrating on the heart, or sometimes more spontaneously without a prompt, the personal heart opens into this deeper heart, resulting in a welling up of love for others, for life, for all of creation. My awakening experience was more non-dual than I first perceived. In any case, I directly experienced a greater level of reality.

Three Levels of Awakening—Head, Heart and Gut

Adyashanti, in *The End of Your World*, speaks of three non-hierarchical levels of awakening—head, heart and gut.[41] You may have experienced awakening on one of these levels and think you've had a full awakening experience, not realizing there are other different forms. My first experience was obviously at the heart level.

If you awaken at the head level, you may experience an openness, spaciousness, emptiness or awareness of the Great Mystery. If you are more heart-centered, you may experience awakening in a more intimate way, feeling a higher presence surrounding you followed by a joy and love for all creation. You may know at your core that love is the source of this joy and guides all that happens to you. At the gut level, you may experience awakening in a more grounded way. Any existential fear of annihilation vanishes. The mature seeker eventually experiences awakening on all three levels in a whole-body, wordless awareness.

When traveling home from an event in a nearby city, R. M. Bucke experienced an awakening mostly on the mind level, but also with elements of the heart.

> All at once, without warning of any kind, I found myself wrapped in a flame-coloured [sic] cloud. For an instant I thought of fire, an immense conflagration somewhere close by in the great city; the next instant I knew that that fire was in myself. Directly afterwards there came upon me a sense of exultation, of immense joyousness, accompanied or immediately followed by an intellectual illumination quite impossible to describe. Among other things, I did not merely come to believe, I saw that the universe is not composed of dead matter, but is, on the contrary, a living Presence; I became conscious in myself of eternal life. It was not a conviction that I would have eternal life, but a consciousness that I possessed eternal life then; I saw that all men [sic] are immortal; that the cosmic order is such that without any peradventure all things work together for the good of each and all; that the foundation principle of the world, of all worlds, is what we call love, and the happiness of each and all is in the long run certain. The vision lasted a few seconds and was gone; but the memory of it and the sense of the reality of it has remained during the quarter of a century which has since elapsed.[42]

Bucke's awakening of the mind yields comforting insights into the laws of the universe. Wouldn't you like to know that love is the underlying foundation of the universe and that your happiness is certain in the long run? Perhaps you have already experienced these truths. At times, I've experienced these universal laws and taken solace from them, especially when life gets rough.

The Sufi tradition mainly focuses on the awakening in the heart. Although HIK advocates a balance between mind and heart, he declares, "Spiritual attainment is to be conscious of the Perfect One, who is formed in the heart."[43] In the *Gayan*, he offers a beautiful description of this awakening.

> I searched but I could not find Thee.
> I called Thee aloud standing on the minaret
> I rang the temple bell at the rising and setting of the sun.
> I bathed in the Ganges in vain.
> I came back from the Kaaba disappointed.
> I looked for Thee on earth.
> I searched for Thee in heaven, my beloved.
> But at last I found Thee,
> Hidden as a pearl in the shell of my heart.[44]

Can you relate to the frustration that spiritual seeking often brings? Like HIK, you may erroneously look for spiritual fulfillment externally instead of being present to what's within you and in this case what's within your heart.

Having not experienced an awakening at the gut level, I can't totally understand it, nor have I come across many writings about it. However, I do have a personal experience that borders on it. During a retreat, I opened to the Greater All, saying I was ready to face my fears. At that moment, an incredible wind suddenly arose, violently shaking my cabin. Cowering, I said, "Maybe I'm not ready to face my fears just yet!" Instantly, to my surprise, the wind subsided. A year or so later, again while I was on a retreat, existential fear arose in my belly. This time, I decided to face it. My experience was so intense that I dropped to the floor, thrashing around until it finally subsided. I have no idea how long this lasted. I knew only that some deep-seated fear had left me—not all fears, though, because some still arise on occasion. I doubt I'd believe this account if I hadn't experienced it myself.

Third Oxherding Picture:
First Glimpse of the Ox

The third Zen Oxherding picture portrays the non-abiding form of awakening—a spontaneous and sudden first glimpse of the ever-present Source. The drawing reveals the Ox's back, not the whole Ox. There's more to come! Nevertheless, the change in perception is great. No longer is ultimate Truth a theoretical concept but rather an actual reality. The commentary states: "If he will but listen intently to everyday sounds, he will come to realization and at that instant see the very Source. The six senses are no different from the Source. In every activity the Source is manifestly present."[45] This illustrates the importance of spiritual practice ("listening to everyday sounds") as a path to awakening. Over time, such practices may lead you to the realization that the Source or Divine is present in all things.

Awakening and/or spiritual experiences occur more often than you think. The Pew Research Center reported in 2009 that 49 percent of Americans said they'd had a religious or mystical experience.[46] This is an impressive and surprising statistic. Such experiences can help you realize the existence of another dimension of reality. They can activate a desire for more of these experiences and motivate you to pursue the spiritual path. But they are not—repeat *not*—necessary for the journey. Without such experiences, you may launch directly into the purification process, discussed in the next chapter, which *is* crucial for real spiritual growth and will most likely lead you to an awakening/spiritual experience at the appropriate time.

Reflections on the Awakening Stage

1. An awakening experience is spontaneous and comes as a grace. You cannot force such an experience, but you can put yourself in a more receptive place to receive such a grace. Examples of receptive activities include spending time in silence, meditating, going on a retreat or walking in nature. Which modality works for you?

2. Look over your life to see if you've had an awakening experience as described in this chapter. What insight came to you? How did it change you?

3. Take some time to be present to your subtle heart at the center of your chest. What does it reveal?

Chapter 5:
Clearing Light–Purification/
Self-Simplification Overview

Enlightenment is a demolition project. It simply tells you that everything you ever believed was true isn't. Everything you take yourself to be, whatever your self-image is—good, bad or indifferent—you're not that. Whatever you think about God is wrong.

–Adyashanti[47]

The dismantling of our false structures is holy work.

–Mirabai Starr[48]

As you recall, the first Oxherding picture states: "Because of his defilements he has lost sight of the Ox."[49] How true! I'm sure you've experienced how distractions such as anxieties, emotional upheavals, childhood wounds, social media, and so much more prevent you from realizing your True Nature. Many traditions offer ways to become free of these hindrances. Christian wisdom defines this process as Purification or Self-Simplification[50], which has two components: releasing and transforming. Buddhist wisdom often refers to this process as detachment. Sufis speak of polishing the mirror of your heart, so it can clearly reflect the divine radiance. Shaman Martin Prechtel describes it as being carved by life into a sufficient shape to be able to enter deeper realities. This image evokes in me a sense of letting go of bulky baggage in order to fit through a narrow opening into a greater reality.[51]

Releasing purification is a stripping away of all that does not serve you—all those superfluous, unreal and harmful things that dissipate your energy. These include addictions, attachment to material things, need for certain outcomes, self-importance, obsessive busyness, distractions, or your ideas about life.

Transforming purification calls for an upgrading and unification of the discordant elements of your being. These may be unhealed traumas, scattered energies, out of control urges and emotions, or disturbing behavioral patterns. They contain some of your vital energy but are stuck in the past and separated from the main energy-stream of your life. If you push them away, you push away some of your life energy. Rather than discarding these parts, it's best to accept and work on transforming them. This releases the stuck energies and brings them into better alignment with your True Nature.

The Purification/Self-Simplification Stage necessitates difficulties, demands and challenges. However, many travelers on the spiritual path would prefer to bypass this arduous, but crucial stage. Some New Age spiritualities completely circumvent it. They promote the idea that you can create anything you want—happiness, money, a fulfilling job, or a beautiful relationship—without much hardship.

The real journey involves the difficult process of freeing yourself—or being freed—from all that is discordant with who you really are.

> To attain to the purity which is the seeking of the mystic one must be able to purify one's spirit from every thought and feeling, however deeply impressed or engraved in one's heart. The mystic goes as far as purifying himself from his identity. . . . From beginning to end the whole process of spiritual development depends upon this.[52]
>
> –HIK, The Gathas

In the Christian tradition, descriptions of the Purification Stage go as far back as the fourth century, appearing in the writings of Gregory of Nyssa (335-395).[53] Here are other examples of purification expressed in the varying wisdom traditions.

- The first terrace of the Mount of Purgatory in Dante's *Divine Comedy* includes the need to let go of pride so as to become humble.[54]

- Sufi poet Attar (1146–1221) in his "Conference of the Birds" calls the first of seven valleys of the spiritual journey "the valley of self-stripping and renunciation."[55]

- Pictures 4 and 5 of the Zen Oxherding pictures—"Catching and Taming the Ox"—address purification in terms of breaking disruptive habits and training the mind to let go of distracting thoughts in meditation.[56]

- Classic Zen literature is filled with stories of masters, who after their awakening retreated to the mountains for decades to process their experience and eliminate any remaining karma or residual hinderances.[57]

If you're serious about your spiritual development, you can't escape the purification process. Most of your time will be spent in this stage. It's a long, slow, arduous but necessary process. As the Hindu saint Anandamayi Ma (1896-1982) said: "Precious gems are profoundly buried in the earth and can only be extracted at the expense of great labor."[58]

Active and Passive Approaches to Purification/ Self-Simplification

Purification or self-simplification can be active or passive. Active purification means you make a conscious decision to purify, giving up something or participating in a self-improvement activity. Active purification can only take you so far. Eventually, you'll need to surrender all your desires—even for spiritual attainment—and allow something greater to direct your life.

Passive purification doesn't have a conscious component; it seemingly happens *to* you. I say seemingly because it may be your deeper self that is creating ways to purify. "It is love in disguise,"[59] as the contemporary spiritual teacher, Amoda Maa, claims. Passive purification can take many forms. You may be forced to become detached by external circumstances—a fire that burns your possessions, the death of a loved one, an illness or accident, a dear friend who moves away or the loss of your livelihood. Sometimes you simply outgrow your attachment. It no longer excites or interests you. Eruptions from your unconscious—such as emotional outbursts, upsetting dreams or inner agitations that cause you to take stock of your life and make changes—are other forms of passive purification. According to John of the Cross, active and passive purification occur on two levels—the physical and the spiritual. He calls passive purification at the spiritual level by a different name—the Dark Night of the Soul. (See Chapter 10).

Purpose

What is the primary purpose of purification? Many self-help articles address the importance of eliminating clutter in your home and offer ways to tackle this chore. Purification or self-simplification addresses getting rid of clutter in your inner home and transforming it into the radiant being you truly are—in other words, to find your True Nature or be united with the Radiant All.

Other benefits from purification can occur before reaching these final states. You may navigate the ups and downs of life more easily. You may find yourself turning away from things that once held your interest and finding joy in new and unexpected places. You may see life from a broader and more open perspective and more frequently experience the ways the Divine permeates your everyday life.

In most cases, this clearing or purification process never ends. You might find that the closer you get toward the goal, the easier it is to see what's standing in your way. It's like shining a light into a dark room and exposing the creepy crawlies in the corners. Some traditions attest that purification continues beyond the grave. For instance, concepts such as purgatory and reincarnation point to a continuation of the purification process after physical death.

Going through this purification/self-simplification process is not about attaining perfection. Adyashanti often likens awakening or becoming enlightened to the Zen *koan* (a riddle that baffles your conceptual mind) in which a bull jumps through a window. The whole bull gets through the window except his tiny tail.[60] Why? For

Adyashanti, the tail represents our humanness. As humans, we have certain flaws that remain unhealed despite our best efforts. Even spiritual masters or saints had flaws. Adyashanti quips that the only real saints or masters are dead ones.[61] Yet, despite these flaws, these high beings opened themselves sufficiently for the Divine to shine through them. Through the purification process, you are released or transformed from most of what no longer serves you, but not everything. The key is to be conscious of your flaws, accept them, and notice what happens. This way, your flaws don't get in the way of your spiritual development.

If you can reach a state of abiding awakening, coming home, or realization of your True Nature without completing the purification process, then why keep purifying? Often you don't have a choice because passive purification—being forced to release something—can occur at any moment. If you do have a choice, why would you continue this difficult process of letting go or transforming?

I think the answer lies in the concept of capacity. I remember a Sunday school teacher speaking about water (the Divine) filling containers of varying sizes. The water fills each one completely, but the larger containers get "more" of the Divine filling. It's a crude metaphor, but I interpret it as supporting the idea that purification creates more capacity. The more you simplify and transform, the more magnetism and light you hold, and consequently, the greater your effect on the world. Rumi, in "Mathnawi," communicates the same idea as my Sunday school teacher.

> The wine of divine grace is limitless:
> All limits come only from the faults of the cup.
> Moonlight floods the whole sky from horizon to horizon;
> How much it can fill your room depends on its windows.[62]

Certain individuals are so purified that they support the whole world. The Sufis speak of the *qutb*, a perfected human being living on earth during every age. This person, unknown to all but a few mystics, is the central axis that holds the world together. The Trappist monk, Thomas Merton (1915–1968) in *New Seeds of Contemplation* expresses a similar idea:

I wonder if there are twenty men [sic] alive in the world now who see things as they really are. That would mean that there were twenty men who were free, who were not dominated or even influenced by any attachment to any created thing or to their own selves or to any gift from God, even the highest, the most supernaturally pure of His graces. I don't believe that there are twenty such men alive in the world. But there must be one or two. They are the ones who are holding everything together and keeping the universe from falling apart.[63]

Here is the answer to why you should keep purifying whether through releasing or transforming—so you can be an increasingly positive influence in the world and aid in its upliftment.

Your Drive and Commitment to the Process

You need a strong drive to persevere during the purification process. An awakening experience can ignite or strengthen this drive. After such an expanded experience, you most likely want more and are willing to undergo the difficulties of the path to get there. However, you can have just as strong a drive without having such a life-changing experience. This drive appears in those who make their spiritual growth the main focus of their lives. Such devotion could take the form of practicing daily meditation, attending retreats or committing to your psychological and spiritual growth. Many serious spiritual seekers I know are relieved to know that an awakening experience is not necessarily an indicator of spiritual progress.

Eventually, the spiritual journey calls for a clearing of even this drive, important as it was up to this point. When you detach from actively seeking your goal and surrender to what is, you align with or sink into the greater Will (Flow of the Universe)—not with your personal will.

I can't explain why the drive to spiritual development is so strong in some people and not in others. Those who believe in reincarnation might say the drive is strong because of past lives of devotion or good behavior. Maybe this is true. I also wonder why some people who have spent years on the spiritual path and who have a strong drive for the releasing and transformative aspects of purification do not have an awakening experience while others who live their life without any particular spiritual practice do experience one. It all remains a mystery to me.

The Dance Between Stages

The separation between purification and illumination—the next stage of the Way—is an artificial construct. In reality, you oscillate or dance between the two stages. You may experience a spiritual expansion that is followed by a contraction. However, if you continue on your path, you most likely will experience more expansions than contractions. You may find yourself living more in the realm of light and less in your constricted ways of being. Underhill uses the metaphor of a baby learning to walk.[64] At first, falls outnumber the moments of staying upright, but slowly the falls lessen until the toddler fully walks.

The next two chapters explore in depth the releasing and the transformation aspects of purification. These are followed by a chapter about how opportunities for purification occur in your everyday life.

Reflections on Purification/Self-Simplification Overview

1. Recall the times when you've experienced passive purification. What was taken away from you? What benefit did you gain from these experiences?

2. Were there any times when you simply outgrew an attachment?

3. When challenging events occur in your life, you could ask yourself if you are too attached to something.

4. How do you balance the need for a strong will to grow spiritually with one that surrenders to your higher or Divine self?

Chapter 6:
Liberating Light–Releasing
and Detachment

Bowing down, "I release all that does not serve me."
Rising up, "I arise to my true self."[65]

This Sufi practice succinctly expresses the process of releasing and its purpose, namely, to liberate your psyche from anything that keeps you from the realization of your True Nature. It includes all your false ideas about life, relationships or yourself. Behaviors that don't align with who you really are, such as trying to please others or being addicted to someone or something, also need releasing. Situations that complicate your life unnecessarily, drain your energy, keep you stuck or block you from your true desires likewise need clearing.

Although stripping away and detachment are both aspects of purification, they aren't always equivalent. Evelyn Underhill defines detachment as being in "right relation to" something or someone. Maybe this means letting go of something, but maybe not. It can simply signify not giving too much importance to it. You could be too attached to your car if you polish it all the time, worry about it getting a scratch, or allow it to boost your ego. Detachment from your car doesn't always mean you should sell it and take public transportation. It simply means using your car as needed without giving it undue importance. Right relationship calls for keeping your priorities straight. You can tell your priorities are out of order if they cause anxiety and worry, take too much of your attention, complicate your life or distract you from your true desires.

Fr. John told me I could journal but warned me not to get too attached to my journaling. I could pray, meditate and even have high spiritual experiences, but I should not get too attached to any of them. Knowing that skipping Sunday Mass is a serious sin in the Catholic Church, I facetiously asked, "If I get too attached to going to Mass, would you tell me to give it up?" To my surprise, he answered, "Yes!" Getting too attached to anything—even a spiritual practice—starts to make the practice more important than its goal.

> If the scissors are not used daily on the beard,
> it will not be long before the beard is, by its luxuriant growth,
> pretending to be the head.
>
> –Hakim Jami (1414–1492), *The Way of the Sufi*[66]

The processes of stripping away, transformation and detachment can occur at different levels of your being. Once you become aware of the stripping away process, you start to see more elements of your life that need releasing. At other times, you may need to upgrade or transform certain parts of you that don't sufficiently align with your True Nature. Sometimes you may need to practice detachment by asking if your priorities are in the right order. Do you place too much or too little emphasis on eating, exercising, spending time at work or engaging in spiritual practices?

Passive purification may happen in all three processes. You might not want to release, transform or detach from something but for some conscious or unconscious reason you're not able to do so. Fierce grace might then arise. Circumstances force you to purify, like it or not!

The following table shows elements in your life that need releasing (stripping away), upgrading (transformation) and other ones that require you to have the right relationship to those essential parts of your life.

Levels and Types Purification

Levels of Being	Strip Away or Transform	Cultivate the Right Relationship to
Physical	Substance abuse, pain, body image	Possessions, food, sleep, exercise
Emotional	Fear, anxiety, anger, worry, hurt, unwanted impulses, guilt, sorrow	Feelings about others, yourself, circumstances
Mental	Programming, obsessions, habits, unhealthy beliefs, distractions	Thoughts, intuition, ideas, knowledge
Personal	Fame, power, self-importance, self-centeredness, self-identities, control, possessiveness	Love relationships, work, play
Spiritual	Control, possessiveness, certain spiritual outcomes	Guide, spiritual experiences (called consolations), spiritual practice, times for prayer

The list could go on almost endlessly. No wonder seekers spend most of their time in this phase of their spiritual growth.

It's possible to become too attached to the idea of detachment. I know one person who sold or gave away her possessions every few months. She spent an enormous amount of time buying new things. This distracted her from paying attention to her spiritual growth. While working with the people living in poverty, another friend became too attached to being poor, thinking it a spiritual necessity. He hesitated to become a priest because it meant living in the "posh" rectory and sleeping in his own room with a nice bed. He was called to serve poor people as a priest, but his attachment to poverty almost blocked him from becoming one.

Stripping away and/or detachment can be—but is not always—a painful process. Suffering the loss of a loved one, enduring an illness, recovering from an accident, giving up your cherished ideas or self-identity—all generate sorrow and pain. While in the hospital after a heart attack and hovering close to death, the psychologist, Carl Jung (1875–1961), in *Memories, Dreams and Reflections* had a vision in which he experienced this painful stripping away.

> As I approached the steps leading up to the entrance into the rock, a strange thing happened: I had the feeling that everything was being sloughed away; everything I aimed at or wished for or thought, the whole phantasmagoria of earthly existence, fell away or was stripped from me—an extremely painful process. Nevertheless, something remained. . . . This experience gave me a feeling of extreme poverty, but at the same time of great fullness. There was no longer anything I wanted or desired. I existed in an objective form.[67]

The Jesuit priest and paleontologist, Pierre Teilhard de Chardin in *Hymn of the Universe* describes his experience of this stripping away as a heavy cloak falling from his shoulders, "the dead weight of all that is false, narrow, tyrannical, all that is artificially contrived, all that is merely human in humanity." As a result, he felt permanently connected to a "greater reality, which was now revealing itself."[68]

The death of Mirabai Starr's daughter when she was fourteen years old created a "tsunami that rearranged the entire landscape of [her] life."[69] Adding to her roles as author and teacher, she became a grief counselor, now understanding the holiness of death and dying and the transformative power of grief and grieving. She describes death as "a portal for some of the most potent and transformative of experiences we can have as human beings."[70]

So, there's a purpose to this often-painful stripping away, namely, to discover your True Nature. Jung called it "objective form;" Teilhard, "greater reality;" Starr, as a portal to "transformative consciousness."

Right Relationship to Distractions

> Where can he have that pure and naked vision of unchange-
> able Truth, who is so busied with other things? [These] operate
> upon his thoughts and imaginations and confuse and enchain
> his mind?[71]

Written by Gelac Petersen in 1616, this passage shows that distractions have been a problem for centuries. The challenge is magnified today with diversions such as social media, texting and so much more. As Peterson notes, distractions confuse, cloud the mind and prevent the seeker from reaching the Great Mystery. Distractions plague not only spiritual seekers but all human beings. Studies show that constant texting or responding to social media can lead to higher levels of depression and stress.[72] Are you one of the many who turn to these distractions to fill an emptiness or resolve boredom only to realize your ploys are just temporary fixes?

Distractions aren't going to disappear. They bombard the meditating mind and prevent your ability to focus. So how can you develop a right relationship to them? Spiritual teachings offer different techniques for working with distractions. These include saying a mantra, repeating a question, visualizing a specific scenario or simply being present to what arises. (See suggestions at the end of this chapter.)

> This is the only meditation I know.
> While I eat, I eat.
> While I walk, I walk.
> And while I feel sleepy, I sleep.
> Whatever happens, happens.
> I never interfere.
>
> –Bokuju[73]

One summer afternoon, I dove down to the bottom of a pool, allowing my full attention to rest there. I heard children playing and laughing somewhere above me, but the deep water between us muffled the sound and didn't disturb my focus. Later, I thought it was a great metaphor for handling distractions in meditation. They are present but of little interest. Sometimes the children rest and eat lunch, which is equivalent to finding yourself in silence as you explore the deep water. This is a delicious place to be! Most of the time, however, thoughts during meditation don't take a nap but can be minimized if you sink below your mind's surface to focus on something deeper.

Once, while on a fourteen-day retreat, my thoughts wouldn't settle at all. I wondered why they remained in full force even without the usual outside distractions. Eventually, I shifted my perspective and viewed them as pesky kids who wanted to come along for the ride. My experience confirmed what spiritual teachers had advised, which is to accept your thoughts without dwelling on them. An apt metaphor is seeing someone pass you on the street without turning around to look at them. It sounds easy but can be extremely challenging.

Often, my thoughts seem to be embedded in a vastness difficult to describe. Words like thereness, goodness, support, love and quiet fullness approximate this experience. It doesn't matter that my thoughts are present because they are eclipsed by the vastness and are just part of the whole. Sometimes, however, a thought is so strong that the vastness fades or disappears. I consider it a grace when I become aware of this diversion. If it's important and needs immediate attention, I concentrate on it and the feelings it evokes. If it's important but not urgent, I write it down and attend to it later.

My teacher once told me, "If you wait for your mind to stop, you're going to wait forever." I suddenly had to rethink my avenue to enlightenment. I'd been trying to stop my mind for a very long time, and I knew I had to find another course of action. The spiritual instruction to "just stop" is not directed to the mind, or to feelings or to the personality. It's directed to the afterthought that takes credit or blame and says, "It's mine."

–Adyashanti, *Emptiness Dancing*[74]

You can react positively or negatively when noticing your mind has gone off on a tangent. You could beat yourself up for straying, or you could see it as a grace which brings you back to center. The distraction is not a grace but noticing the distraction is a grace. It gives you the opportunity for you to return to your practice.

Freedom from Results

The Need to Win

When an archer is shooting for nothing
He has all his skill.
If he shoots for a brass buckle
He is already nervous.
If he shoots for a prize of gold
He goes blind
Or sees two targets—
He is out of his mind!

His skill has not changed. But the prize
Divides him. He cares.
He thinks more of winning
Than of shooting—
And the need to win
Drains him of power.

–Merton, *Way of Chuang Tzu*[75]

The Bhagavad Gita (2:47) eloquently expresses the importance of letting go of the results of your actions. "Set thy heart on thy work, but never on its reward."[76] If you think about it, the desire for a reward for your work comes from your ego, which likes the positive strokes it gets. If you are in touch with your radiant True Nature, it doesn't matter if the outcome of your work is positive or negative. You're okay no matter what the result. Ironically, a positive outcome is more likely if you don't think about the results but concentrate all your energy on the work at hand. This way, you're not dividing your energy between your work in the present and your desire for a certain outcome in the future.

As a student, I dove into my studies with relatively little care about what would be on the test. I loved learning the material for its own sake. Although I wasn't completely indifferent to the outcome like a true renunciate, I experienced more peace when I dispensed with the results. I had inadvertently discovered the spiritual tenet of letting go of results.

Right Relationship to Self-Identities

Part of the purification process requires that you not overly identify with your roles in life—parent, teacher, spouse, helper, professional, achiever or spiritual person—settling there, rather than seeing the deeper and more expansive you, which lies beneath all roles. You don't have to give up any of these identities, but rather have a right relationship to them. This means realizing that these identities don't define you. They are merely aspects of you, not who you truly are. You probably know people who put all their energy into a certain identity. For example, a mother might feel lost when her children go off to college, a helper might not know who she is if she isn't helping someone, or a person might feel useless if he's not doing something to make the world a better place. All these are noble pursuits as long as they don't mask the real you, as long as you realize that your core self still exists even when these identities diminish.

When you are liberated from defining yourself in terms of your identities, you realize that you're not a spiritual person, nor a great meditator, nor a great helper, but simply yourself. It's so compelling to latch onto an identity, such as "I am a spiritual person," but the goal is to be free of all identities and just be you.

This mirrors Rabbi Susya's saying: "In the world to come I will not be asked why I was not Moses, I will be asked why I was not Susya."[77] Like Rabbi Susya, Fr. John, my first spiritual director, told me not to expect that I would become like St. Francis, Jesus, St. Teresa or any other spiritual being. He emphasized that I couldn't consciously know who or what was the real me. He conveyed the spiritual principle that if you have a set idea of who you'll be, you might strive to become a false self or some idealized self-image (accompanied by a lot of "shoulds") rather than allow the real you to arise organically from your very depths.

A member of my spiritual community remarked how strongly she identified with herself as a singer. Even as a baby, she sang notes rather than cry. Sometimes her parents listened to her in wonder, momentarily forgetting to attend her needs. Now that she's aging, she has lost most of her voice's range and quality. She never knows if a song will come out in a rough or sweet voice. This required her to give up most of her singing groups. For now, she has found solace in joining the Threshold Choir—a group that sings comforting and soothing songs for people who are ill or dying. The musical range of these songs is narrow and sometimes members just hum. This beautiful solution to an aging voice gently encourages her to release her identity as a singer. It helps her to look more deeply into who she truly is. Of course, at some point her singing voice will most likely be gone. Perhaps, by that time it won't matter, because she will have found her true, radiant nature, which is beyond all self-identities.

After a long retreat, my identity as a spiritual seeker disappeared. I don't know how that happened. I simply realized that I could no longer think of myself as spiritual. This sent me into a tailspin for months because I truly believed "spiritual" was who I was. It superseded my identities as wife, mother, teacher and spiritual guide. I found myself in the Dark Wood Stage, feeling empty and bereft. My guide suggested I observe what was happening around me. If the results of my presence were beneficial to those around me, then I had not fallen off the wagon but had progressed on my journey. I found this to be helpful guidance. Those around me were in fact benefitting from my interactions with them even though I felt empty inside. Now I see myself as simply Alice, although I cannot articulate who or what she is. Yes, I am still a wife, mother, teacher, writer and guide, but those identities don't define me. I find it liberating. It's taken me a long time to reach this place and it hasn't been easy. Perhaps I needed to experience these many identities before realizing there is something deeper within me that holds them all.

Calling Card

Keichu, the great Zen teacher of the Meiji era, was the head of Tofuku, a cathedral in Kyoto. One day the governor of Kyoto called upon him for the first time.

His attendant presented the card of the governor, which read: Kitagaki, Governor of Kyoto.

"I have no business with such a fellow," said Keichu to his attendant. "Tell him to get out of here."

The attendant carried the card back with apologies. "That was my error," said the governor, and with a pencil he scratched out the words Governor of Kyoto. "Ask your teacher again."

"Oh, is that Kitagaki?" exclaimed the teacher when he saw the card. "I want to see that fellow."

–*Zen Flesh, Zen Bones*[78]

Freedom from Your Stories/Beliefs

So much of our suffering results from the stories and interpretations we create around events. The emotional or physical pain of these events is real, but the stories around them make them worse. You might think God doesn't love you, or that something happened because you are flawed at your very core, or that you are being punished for your transgressions. Such stories and related beliefs often imprint so deeply on you that they create similar repeating situations in your life. How does this happen?

Your understanding of a life event causes you to take certain actions. These behaviors produce a result that in turn reinforces your belief. For example, if you believe you're not good enough, you'll try harder to live up to higher, almost impossible standards, only to fall short of them. This confirms you're not good enough. Becoming aware of and changing your actions—such as refusing an attempt to meet impossible standards—breaks the cycle and produces a different result.

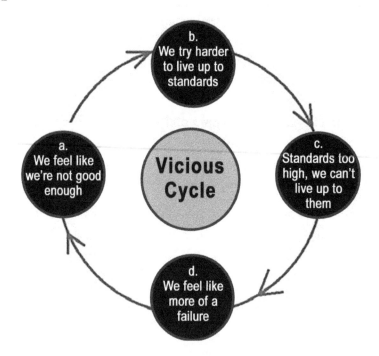

The beliefs that cause repeating situations in your life often stem from childhood experiences buried in your unconscious. For example, Scott Peck in *The Road Less Traveled* tells of a client named Stewart who claimed to be an atheist. Stewart suffered from a pain he described as a knife cutting his throat. He had gone to many doctors who found no physiological explanation for the pain. After several therapy sessions, Peck helped Stewart realize that at some deep level he believed in a God who would punish him, who would cut his throat because of some misdeeds he had committed as a teenager. This realization healed his throat pain.[79] If you can unearth these unconscious beliefs, discover their underlying source/trauma and heal them, you break the harmful cycle.

You may become too attached to your beliefs or concepts about spirituality or how the world works, mistaking them for Reality itself. Even the process of naming objects removes you from the actual experience of it. Saying "that's a flower" narrows your experience of its indescribable essence. Philosopher Alfred North Whitehead (1861–1947) calls it "the fallacy of misplaced concreteness."[80] You mistake the concept for the true reality. Zen *koans*—baffling stories, statements or questions—intentionally help you let go of your ideas about reality so you can directly experience it. Mystic Howard Thurman (1900–1981) advocates "listening for the sound of the genuine."[81] This practice also helps you let go of your stories and mental constructs and connects you with a deeper Reality.

The story about Yamaoka-san shows how learning about spiritual concepts can miss the real truth.

Nothing Exists

Yamaoka Tesshu, as a young student of Zen visited one master after another. He called upon Dokuon of Shokoku.

Desiring to show his attainment, he said: "The mind, Buddha and sentient beings, after all, do not exist. The true nature of phenomena is emptiness. There is no realization, no delusion, no sage, no mediocrity. There is no giving and nothing to be received."

Dokuon, who was smoking quietly, said nothing. Suddenly he whacked Yamaoka with his bamboo pipe. This made the youth quite angry.

"If nothing exists," inquired Dokuon, "where did this anger come from?"

–*Zen Flesh, Zen Bones*[82]

Yamaoka-san had absorbed many ideas about Zen but failed to grasp the underlying energy from which all things—including anger—arise.

Freedom from your Ego Desires

The Buddhist Second Noble Truth proclaims that the cause of suffering is egoic desires, cravings or attachments. The Third Noble Truth asserts that cessation of desires, cravings or attachments ends suffering. John of the Cross, in *Ascent of Mount Carmel*, concurs with the Buddhist view when he proclaims the best way to purify is to release all desires.

To attain to enjoyment of all things,
Desire to enjoy none.
To attain to knowledge of all things,
Desire to know nothing of any.
To attain to possession of all things,
Desire to possess none.
To become everything,
Desire to be nothing.[83]

In contrast, the Sufi perspective, as stated by HIK, advocates transforming rather than stripping away your desires. He claims all desires contain divine energy: "To repress desire is to repress a divine impulse (*Gayan*)."[84] He claims, "we can be bound by desires, yet we cannot live without them."[85] At the same time, all desires are not equal. It could be bowling on Wednesday nights, country walks or spiritual bliss. These are not necessarily exclusive. Bowling might give you more spiritual bliss and a better sense of reality than some spiritual practices.

You can't try to upgrade your desires if you're not ready. If you do, it becomes a "should" rather than a natural, true desire. You might say your desire is to spend more time meditating, but in actuality you'd rather do something else with that time.

How then do you enhance a desire without it becoming a "should?" You may simply become bored or grow out of a desire (passive purification). Taking a more active stance, you may focus on the deepest longing in your heart—your deepest desire—and see where your lesser desires land. Eventually, your deepest desire will be to relinquish all desires, as noted by John of the Cross, and thus "become everything."

Right Relationship to Your Egoic Self: Surrender

Detachment from your ego is the deepest and most difficult part of the purification process. Again, this is not about giving up your egoic self but having the right relationship to it. No one wants the paintbrush to create a picture, and yet the artist needs the paintbrush to implement his creation. Similarly, the ego is needed to carry out the wishes of your

True Nature. Ideally, it should take orders from the true you. Unfortunately, the ego often wants to run the show.

Surrendering to the Divine within or beyond you helps you achieve the right relationship to your ego so it doesn't rule your life. It asks you to acquiesce each moment to the Radiant All, to what is. Amoda Maa defines surrender as open-heartedness. It is "what remains when there is no attempt to fix anything."[86] Surrender ushers you to a place of greater reality, but it's not easy.

At one point I discovered that I often mess up when left to my own devices. For example, if I push too hard for a specific outcome, it often falls apart. One time I diligently wrote a series of grants to raise money for building the lodge at our retreat center. Only one small grant came through, but substantial money came to us in unexpected ways without any effort on my part. These and other incidents forced me to realize that Something Greater than my conscious self was running the show and it was doing a much better job than me.

I've learned to trust this Greater All. As Julian of Norwich (1343-1416) claims: "All will be well, and every kind of thing will be well."[87] It's not easy to believe her words. It has taken decades for me to develop trust that all will be well in the end, and sometimes I rail against it.

Meister Eckhart tells the story of a man who totally surrendered to the greater Reality. He never had a bad day because no matter what happened he would praise God. He was never unhappy because he believed that anything that happened to him was God's will and his only desire was to live in God's will.[88] His was a high level of surrender, which created ongoing happiness.

I couldn't relate to this story until I thought of the times when a new love—an intimate partner or a newborn baby—came into my life. At these times, the love was so strong that it overshadowed any daily hassles. Imagine that your boss could admonish you for some error, but it would hardly affect you because you knew you were going to see your new love that evening. You wouldn't mind feeding your baby in the middle of the night or changing her diapers because your open heart overshadowed any inconvenience.

Adyashanti in *Falling into Grace* claims that personal suffering is caused by wanting things to be different, by arguing with what is, and by trying to control reality.[89] It follows that surrendering to whatever is happening eliminates these three causes of suffering. If you truly accept what's occurring at any moment, then you wouldn't want things to be different; you wouldn't argue with or try to change this reality. Such a task is not easy and demands a high level of spiritual development.

To be clear, surrender does not mean being a doormat or allowing abuse or injustice. It's not a surrender to a person, but to the Divine within you. In these situations, your deepest self might suddenly erupt from within you and say "No!" Jesus driving the money changers from the temple (Matthew 21:12–17)[90] cogently models this needed response.

How do you reach a place of surrender in abuse or unjust situations where you have no control? Can you trust that what happens to you is for the best, that a loving hand is behind it all even though it's a tough loving hand? Such a tall order requires tremendous trust—not a blind faith, but one based on experience. Looking over the difficulties in your life and observing how they helped you grow is a way to strengthen this trust. Perhaps you gained some wisdom or other gift from these ordeals.

At times, I would experience a "loving hand" behind a trying situation *after* it had passed. During difficult times I might intellectually know there's a beneficence behind what I'm experiencing, but I couldn't feel it. I'd grumble and complain and certainly could not praise like the man in Eckhart's story. Although it's not easy, most of the time I now see difficult times as a way to surrender my will to the greater Will, to the greater flow of the universe. It may take time to understand the reason why these challenges occur, but I surrender anyway. In doing so, I feel a softening within me because I'm no longer fighting with reality. This doesn't mean I don't do something about a trying situation if I sense it's the greater Will to do so.

The mystics concur that a loving hand *is* behind all difficulties. In this passage by German mystic Johannes Tauler (1300–1361), God is the one speaking.

> Learn that My Divine nature never worked so nobly in human
> nature as by suffering; and because suffering is so efficacious,

it is sent out of great love. I understand the weakness of human nature at all times, and out of love and righteousness, I lay no heavier load on man than he can bear.[91]

This is the fourteenth-century equivalent of tough love. When my children would receive a painful immunity shot or have stitches, they didn't know it was for their greater good. It only hurt. Is this also true for life's painful experiences? Amoda Maa uses the image of an open hand to denote surrender to whatever arises. She, like many spiritual teachers, affirms that love is behind all difficulties and consequently invites you to accept with an open heart everything that comes your way. "What is broken is the doorway to gold. What is shattered is the entrance to inconceivable love. What brings you to your knees is not a punishment but God's invitation. Your brokenness is holy."[92]

At times, seeing a loving hand behind these sufferings is a hard pill for me to swallow, even though I've seen the benefits. At this point, I am comforted by the words attributed to the late Ram Dass who said. "It's perfect and it sucks."[93] Yes, it's both. From the soul's perspective it's perfect; it's the higher will. But from human viewpoint, it sucks. Sometimes it's difficult for the human part of us to see the perfection until what caused the brokenness is first healed. The next chapter outlines a variety of ways for mending such situations.

Optimally, if you can't change what's happening to you, you could surrender to the all-pervasive love in the universe—but not to any institution or persons that may oppress you. With your heart open—in this way and with love flowing through it—difficult situations become less important. Rather than concentrating on what you've lost or can't change, you can put energy into moving toward love.

Role of Your Will

Cultivating a strong will helps you maintain focus and prevents you from getting swayed by distractions. It makes it possible for you to withstand the powerful energies of higher consciousness. At the same time, releasing your will and surrendering to the greater Will (Flow of the Universe) propels you along the path. How do you reconcile the two?

Ancient wisdom provides a clue. Seekers could not enter Plato's Academy until they were forty years old. The Jewish Kabbalah adhered to the same requirement. These prerequisites underscore the need to develop your will before giving it up. A strong sense of self is a necessary foundation for spiritual growth. Otherwise, you may get overwhelmed by the higher energies or succumb to ego-inflation.

Does this mean that young people today should not devote themselves to spiritual endeavors? Of course not. Unlike ancient times, there aren't any rules preventing young people from pursing their spiritual growth. They may have already developed their will sufficiently or simply felt an inner calling to pursue their spiritual life now. They may have experienced sufficient trauma or suffering, like I did, to ask the greater questions about life.

Renounce and Enjoy

Ironically, this stripping away process allows you to enjoy life more fully. Attachments and distractions no longer divert your attention away from relishing life. Underhill claims the goal of detachment is selfless use, not selfish abuse, of lovely and natural things. This means enjoying these things but not being overly attached to them or wanting certain outcomes from them. You don't have to give these up but have the right relationship to them. St. Augustine makes a similar but more radical statement: "Love and do what you will."[94] This makes sense if you think about it. If you really love, you wouldn't harm others; you wouldn't put yourself above others or hoard your possessions.

When a reporter asked Gandhi if he could sum up his philosophy in a few words, he replied: "Renounce and enjoy."[95] From reading this chapter, you know renouncing or purification is not easy, but it does point the way to greater freedom and enjoyment.

Reflections on Purification as Stripping Away and Detachment

1. You could look over certain difficult events in your life and explore where passive purification happened. From your new perspective, do you see the grace in it?

2. You could list the things in your present life that take energy away from your true purpose—unnecessary things that distract you or take up your time but are really not satisfying. What can you do to lessen these and increase what is truly worthwhile?

3. What are your stories or beliefs about your life? Repeatedly concentrating on the question, "Who am I without my stories and beliefs?" or "Who am I without my personal history?" brings you closer to who you really are.

4. What vicious circles have you created in your life? You can discover them by finding similar, unwanted events that keep repeating. You can then discern what unconscious belief underlies them and what actions you take as a result of this belief. You could change the actions stemming from it, thus breaking the cycle.

5. You could choose one of the following ways to work with distractions:

   a. Practice mindfulness. If you can totally concentrate on whatever presents itself at any given moment in time and let go of thoughts about the past or future, your distractions will no longer disturb you.

   b. Ask yourself a repeating question such as: "What is happening now?" or "What is Truth?" or "What is enlightenment?" This is called inquiry. You can choose what question works best for you. The question keeps you on track and you may find you go deeper each time you ask it.

c. Imagine your thoughts as clouds, which simply float away or put them onboard a passing train. You could think of your thoughts as waves in the ocean which gradually move deeper toward the peaceful ocean floor.

d. During meditation, write down any important thoughts or feelings that arise. This way, you can let go of them right then and attend to them once your meditation finishes.

e. If a disturbing emotion or sensation arises, ask if it can wait until the end of your practice. If the answer is yes, leave it for later. If the answer is no, concentrate on it until it shifts and then return to your meditation.

Chapter 7:
Renewing Light–Purification
as Transformation

Beautiful are those
whose brokenness
gives birth to
transformation and wisdom.

–John Mark Green[96]

Releasing purification focuses on freedom from everything that no longer serves you. Transformation, the second basic way to purify, focuses on those permanent parts of you that still contain your energy but need upgrading or restoration. Although you might want to get rid of some of these parts, such as a pesky inner critic, you would lose vital energy in the process. Transforming this energy into something that aligns more completely with your True Nature prevents such a loss. This transformation can be active or passive. You can work at nurturing and unifying your scattered energies, or it can happen to you through grace.

Some of your energy may be tied up in past traumas, causing you to dissociate or disconnect from the present moment. Healing these traumas frees the confined energy and incorporates it back into you. This released energy can now support you in your growth, so you won't be stuck in the past. Alternatively, your energy might be scattered in different directions, preventing you from moving forward in a way you would like. Unifying these energies helps you progress more easily.

You could also experience opposing desires that prevent you from attaining your goal. You may suddenly become very hungry in the middle of your meditation. Your consciousness is divided between wanting to meditate and wanting to get something to eat. Yet, stripping away hunger is not an option. What's needed is a way to transform your urge to eat so the urge no longer bothers you at the wrong time.

This is not to say that your hunger or any other sensual cravings are bad or sinful, as some theologies claim. They carry divine energy. They become a problem when they take control and fall out of alignment with the vastness of your True Nature—when, as Underhill states, "they have usurped a place beyond their station."[97]

Fourth Oxherding Picture:
Catching the Ox

The commentary to the fourth Oxherding picture addresses both the need for discipline and the difficulty of breaking your habits and conditionings.

> He must tightly grasp the rope and not let it go,
> For the Ox still has unhealthy tendencies.
> Now he charges up to the highlands,
> Now he loiters in a misty ravine.[98]

The ox "still has a tendency to go off on unhealthy tangents. It is unbridled and stubborn."[99] I'm sure you've experienced the tremendous will power needed to break an unhealthy tendency. How easy it is to fall back into your old ways. You might suddenly experience an intense desire for a bowl of ice cream even though you're on a diet, or a desire to stay up late surfing the internet even though you need sleep. These desires pull you away from the longing of your deeper self and prevent your energy from sinking into your True Nature. The transformation techniques explained later in this chapter will help upgrade these desires into ones more in alignment with your True Nature.

Fifth Oxherding Picture:
Taming the Ox

The fifth picture specifically speaks to the taming of the mind. Even if seekers have tamed most of their mind's wayward propensities, they still need to remain vigilant. If you've ever observed your mind during meditation, you know how difficult it is to tame. With practice, however, your deeper mind can become quiet and calm.

> He must hold the nose-rope tight and not allow the Ox to roam,
> lest off to muddy haunts it should stray.
> Properly tended, it becomes clean and gentle,
> Untethered, it willingly follows its master.[100]

Hazrat Inayat Khan beautifully expresses the same thought.

The mind is just like a restive horse. Bring a wild horse and yoke it to a carriage is such a frightening experience for it will kick and jump and run and try to destroy the carriage. . . . When once the mind is disciplined by concentration, by the power of will, then the mind becomes your servant. And once mind has become your servant, then what more do you wish? Then your world is your own. You are king of your kingdom.[101]

The previous chapter discussed ways to let go of distracting thoughts which are byproducts of the mind. These can be stripped away. The taming of the mind is a deeper process. You can't let go of your mind. Rather it needs to be transformed through concentration and willpower.

Training/Discipline and Nurturing of the Self

During medieval times, the taming of the mind and body was called mortification. Seekers used hair shirts, waistbands of nails, whips and excessive fasting to beat into submission the ego's desire for power, control or recognition, and the body's desire for food, sex or comfort. Some spiritual sects still use whips today. Underhill notes that the practitioner often received guidance about when to stop such practices. I'm not sure that mitigates such a brutal way of submission. Meister Eckhart agrees:

> There is a better way to treat one's passions than to pile on oneself ascetic practices which so often reveal a great ego and create more, instead of less, self-consciousness. If you wish to discipline the flesh and make it a thousand times subject, then place on it the bridle of love.[102]

A somewhat milder form of control over bodily cravings happens during athletic training. Athletes tolerate and overcome tiredness and pain to reach their personal best. Such measures develop the will and control bodily urges. In coaching men's downhill ski racing, John McBride required trainees to solve math problems while submerged in ice-cold water—a Navy Seal exercise.[103] I'm no judge of the effectiveness of this method, but it comes close to the caustic mortification practices of earlier times. Fortunately, most athletic training doesn't go to these extreme lengths to tame the body. I agree with Meister Eckhart that although these practices help develop the will, they concurrently strengthen the ego. There's a better way to grow spiritually and that is through opening to love.

Some Zen retreats approach transformation through practices that involve hardship and endurance. Zen practitioners are encouraged to tolerate long periods of pain when sitting in lotus position during meditation or on their legs during talks and meals. While living in Japan many years ago, I attended my first traditional Rinzai Zen retreat. During meditation with my eyes slightly open as instructed, I gasped in fear when I saw the *roshi*'s (senior teacher's) shadow on the wall in front of me with raised stick (*kotsu*) in hand ready to whack anyone who slouched in their posture through lack of sleep or concentration.

It is said that some practitioners become enlightened with the crack of the stick, but I'm sure others suffer from this approach. To be fair, the *roshi* only struck seasoned students, but I didn't know this at the time. I can understand why the *kotsu* is called the encouragement stick since it keeps you alert and can be an instrument for change but seeing it for the first time terrified me and even so, I'm not convinced it's the best approach for spiritual development. During meals, I noticed the *roshi*'s disgust at us beginners because we shifted our legs to the side to alleviate the pain of sitting on them. According to him, we did not have the will to endure the pain needed to tame the body.

Now

I had just one desire—to give myself completely to God. So I headed for the monastery. An old monk asked me, "What is it you want?"
I said, "I just want to give myself to God."
I expected him to be gentle, fatherly, but he shouted at me, "NOW!" I was stunned. He shouted again, "NOW!" Then he reached for a club and came after me. I turned and ran. He kept coming after me, brandishing his club and shouting, "Now. Now."
That was years ago. He still follows me, wherever I go. Always that stick, always that "NOW!"

—Theophane, the Monk, *Tales of the Magic Monastery*[104]

Athletes, and those who meditate, practice active purification of bodily urges, but many individuals experience passive purification that transforms through illness or accidents. For instance, a person may be forced to withstand the pain of a high fever, a broken bone or chemotherapy. If the purpose of active training or endurance is to tame the body, what is the purpose of passive purification? It helps reveal and reinforce the understanding that you're more than your body and, if intense enough, such undesired pain can bring you into a higher state of consciousness.

While intense discipline and training is one approach to transformation, a gentler approach embraces transformation through love.

Tibetan-American Lama Tsultrum Allione teaches a process she calls *Feeding Your Demons*[105] in a book by the same name. The process is based on her revision of the eleventh century Chöd practice created by a female Buddhist teacher, Machig Labdron (1055–1149). A demon is anything that obstructs you from connecting with your True Nature. There are demons of illness, fear, addiction, abuse and egocentricity, to name a few. Her method offers a way to nurture rather than battle these demons. The practitioner asks the demon a series of questions to uncover what it wants, what it needs and how it would feel if it got what it needed. Once this is ascertained, the practitioner imagines feeding the demon with this feeling until it dissolves or transforms into an ally.

For example, suppose the demon is your inner critic. It might *want* you to shape up and behave in a better way. When asked what it needs, it might say it *needs* to be seen and heard. When asked how it would feel if it was really seen and heard, it might say peaceful or supported. You would then imagine a nectar of peace coming through you to the demon and watch what happens. In some cases, it might shrink or disappear, in others it might transform into an ally or helper. No matter what the outcome, the energy that was held by the demon is not lost—it is transformed and integrated back into you. I've found this to be a very powerful practice.

Depending on the situation and your temperament, you may use a more willful or a more nurturing approach to taming unwanted tendencies. HIK strikes a middle way. If a craving—for food, drink, sex, social media—should arise, he suggests waiting twenty minutes before fulfilling it. This prevents you from immediately giving in to these cravings and simultaneously helps you gain discipline and develop your will. At the same time, it doesn't totally deprive you of your cravings. It's a kinder and gentle approach to taming your bodily urges.

Techniques for Transformation

In addition to feeding your demons, many other techniques help transform old wounds, negative feelings, unwanted urges or wayward energies that don't align with your True Nature.

Meditation and **Prayer** are the most widely recognized approach to facilitate transformation. It can take many forms such as a one-pointed concentration on the breath, a word (mantra), phrase, sound or image. Mindfulness, a popular practice today, simply asks you to concentrate on what you're sensing and feeling in the present moment. Meditation can take the form of inquiry in which the practitioner asks a repeated question such as "Who or what am I?" or "What is enlightenment?"

At first, unwelcome thoughts or emotions may surface. They don't show up to annoy or frustrate you (although this may happen), but to help you release them. You could show them acceptance and love as a way to transform them, or they may be released without any effort on your part. Many years ago, my husband and I attended a spiritual initiation ceremony during which we both experienced an intense influx of energy. Upon leaving, we noticed how irritable and crabby we were. Still feeling out of sorts the next day, we went to a nearby beach and a sudden wind picked up. To our amazement, the wind quickly blew away our negativity. We palpably experienced how meditation—or in this case initiation—can bring unwanted tendencies to the surface so they can be cleared. If they had stayed buried in our unconscious, this clearing wouldn't have happened.

Prayer serves as another type of transformation. It shifts your consciousness from your problems and worries to an uplifting state of calm or hope.

Sometimes
when it is all, finally,
too much,
I climb into my car,
roll the windows up,
and somewhere between
backing out the driveway
and rounding the first corner,
I let out a yell
that would topple Manhattan.
How do you pray?

–Margaret Mitchell, *The Feminine Face of God*[106]

Breathing practices provide a powerful way to facilitate transformation and help manage unwanted cravings and tendencies. As HIK says:

> People who become impulsive, or show irritability in nature, who become impatient at times, who get fits of anger, passion or laughter, who get spells of tears, all have an irregularity of breathing as the cause of all this. [T]he mystics of old have for years . . . found in the end that balance of mind entirely depends upon regularity of breathing.[107]

Many spiritual traditions attest to the central role of the breath for self-transformation. Among other techniques, Yogis and Sufis use pranayama (alternate nostril breathing), and Zen offers the counting of the breaths. Christian contemplatives concentrate on a Biblical passage (*lectio divina*), and Jewish mystics focus on the Hebrew letters. These techniques naturally slow down the breath. Holistic healers use conscious breathing techniques such as breathing deeply into various parts of the body. Changing your breath changes your consciousness.

Steady, calm breathing balances the sympathetic and parasympathetic nervous systems, bringing them back into a natural rhythm. Deep breathing distributes energy to all parts of the body, breaking up blocks and activating flow much like acupuncture does. It aids in quieting the mind, which enables your meditative practice to deepen.

The Secret

There was in India a man called Rama Muti. He could lift elephants and stop motorcars running at full speed.
When this man, who was not extraordinary in build, was asked where he got this gigantic strength—for he looked like an ordinary human being, not like a monster—he said, "You know, and yet you do not know. The secret lies in the breath, which is all power."[108]

–Khan, *Tales*

Active imagination[109] is a technique for connecting with various parts of your psyche by using your creativity. It is a valuable tool for healing hurtful experiences or milder forms of trauma. Although you can't change what happened to you in the past, active imagination can help you change the effect of that experience on your psyche. Your body/mind often can't tell the difference between something you imagined and something that actually happened. For example, you can lie in bed perfectly safe when you hear a noise that scares you. Immediately, the adrenal glands start sending cortisol throughout the body, which makes you jumpy and tense even when there's nothing there. Similarly, if you imagine sucking a lemon, your saliva starts to flow, and you might sense a sour taste in your mouth. Your body is reacting solely to your thoughts. In like manner, you can use active imagination to positively change the effect of past hurts on both your body and your psyche.

Sometimes I use active imagination in my work with clients who are experiencing a difficult situation or mild trauma arising from the past. I may ask them to picture light, a higher being, an angel or their adult self in this difficult or traumatic scene and observe what happens without interfering in any way. In most cases, the scene transforms into something less terrifying.

One time, a woman came to see me with sores all over her legs. She had seen several doctors with no improvement. I asked her to be present to the sores on her legs and as she did, an image arose of herself as an eight-year-old. She was in a hospital crib following a tonsillectomy and was angry that her mother was not present. She railed against being put in a bed for babies. Mothers weren't allowed to stay with their children at that time—an antiquated and psychologically damaging practice. I suggested that she imagine her adult-self standing next to the crib and speaking to her child-self with soothing and comforting words. The scene changed. Anger and fear transformed into feelings of warmth and love. Amazingly, her sores disappeared shortly thereafter, illustrating the power of active imagination.

Another time, thirty minutes before I was to conduct my first group retreat, someone rushed up to me declaring there had been a fire in the cottage where she was staying. She had put her clothes on the small propane heater and left the room. I hurried down to see the damage and recoiled at what I saw. One room was covered with soot, the window frames twisted and the mattress charred and dragged outside. I took my own advice about active imagination and imagined an angel present in that room. I felt an angel had indeed been present because the intense fire was confined to only one room. Almost immediately, my anxiety lifted. This simple process allowed me to begin the group retreat with calm and focus, leaving the work of restoration to another day.

Forgiveness, one of the most profound ways of letting go, is another compelling tool for transformation and for healing both psychological and physical hurts. When you carry any kind of resentment, your body tenses and blocks the flow of energy, possibly creating illness or unease. Forgiveness doesn't excuse a person's wrong or hurtful actions. Forgiveness is for you, the forgiver, not for the one being forgiven. It releases you from animosity and resentment, and clears any energetic blocks they may have caused. This enables you to live more fully in the present.

Early in our work together, Fr. John gave me a practice called the Forgiveness Prayer. I began each session with the first part of the "Our Father" until I reached the phrase: "Forgive us our trespasses as we forgive those who trespass against us." For ten minutes, starting with the present moment and going back in time, I recalled people who hurt me and forgave them or set an intention to forgive them if I wasn't ready to do so at that moment. The following day, I would resume where I left off. At the end of each remembered year, I wrote down the date in my journal until I reached the point of imagining myself back in the womb. Ways I had hurt others also surfaced as I returned to each year, showing a need to forgive myself. The process took three months, and I emerged with a sense of lightness and freedom. I've guided others through this exercise and witnessed how even their faces and postures change. Forgiveness is a compelling tool for transformation.

Chakra work[110] generates transformation. The seven major chakras are vortexes of energy placed at different points on your spinal column that affect the energy flow in your body. To increase the flow of energy in the chakras, which in turn connects to the health of the body and psyche, some seekers chant specific vowel sounds or imagine light in each chakra. Others simply concentrate on each chakra, often feeling a warmth, a vibration or an influx of energy in the process. Working with the chakras helps you connect with different facets of your being. As you deepen such work, the psychological needs for fulfillment, control, power or self-importance fall away because the flow of vital energy through your opened chakras leaves you feeling powerful and fulfilled. With practice and without forcing, you may experience a *kundalini* awakening caused by the movement of energy from the root chakra at the base of the spine up and out through the crown chakra.

How does working with your chakras transform bodily urges? Using the chakra system, the leaders at the Thomas Merton Center for Contemplative Prayer developed a technique for transforming ill-timed sexual energy into feelings of compassion.[111] In a meditative state, you imagine a fountain inside you that flows up your body from the second chakra, which is located three vertebrae up from the bottom of the spine, to the fourth chakra located at the heart center. In seconds, the visualization can shift the energy from "I want you" (second chakra) to "What can I do for you?" (fourth chakra). This technique is grounded in several scriptural passages, including Jesus's words to the Samarian woman at the well.

> Whoever drinks this water will get thirsty again; But anyone who drinks the water that I shall give will never be thirsty again; the water that I shall give will turn into a spring inside him, welling up to eternal life. (John 4:13–14)[112]

Because this technique can be powerful, working with a spiritual guide is advised if you practice it regularly.

In addition to a full *kundalini* experience, another goal of chakra work is to become master of your energies so you can direct them as needed at any given moment. In this way, you control your energies rather than remain at their mercy. For example, you can decide to engage your sexual energies during appropriate intimate moments and close them at unsuitable times. This prevents you from desperately seeking an outlet for your sexual urges when intimacy with a loved one is not possible. When you need grounding, you could concentrate on opening the first chakra located at the base of the spine. When you need to communicate well, you could concentrate on the fifth chakra, and so forth. The transformative power of the chakras helps you draw upon the life force within you and direct it in a way that aligns with your true desires.

Pendulation and Shaking are related techniques for countering the negative effects of trauma. Developed by Peter Levine in his book *Waking the Tiger: Healing Trauma*[113], pendulation involves going back and forth between the traumatic event and a place of safety, focusing especially on where each one resides in your body. Periodically returning to a safe place helps you approach the trauma gradually and not be overcome by emotionally charged memories.

Levine highlights the natural instincts of animals when they experience trauma. In particular, he observes how they shake after they experience a threatening event. Studies show that shaking tells the brain to turn off adrenaline, cortisol and/or opioids that are no longer needed after the trauma has passed. Shaking also signals the brain to boost the calming chemicals, such as serotonin, which decrease during trauma. It also releases the deep tension in the large muscles and calms the nervous system.

Most humans stop their natural shaking after a disturbing event because they don't want to look foolish. My friend learned about the importance of shaking shortly before being told she had breast cancer. Not caring how she appeared in front of her doctor after she received the news, she allowed herself to shake vigorously. When the shaking subsided, she became calm and was able to think clearly about a plan for healing.

In *Trauma Releasing Exercises,* David Berceli[114] developed a series of practices that induce shaking. He has used this method all over the world to bring healing and restore balance to both children and adults who suffered trauma. I've found these exercises to be helpful even with minor anxieties and tension. They restore me to a calm, more centered place.

EMDR (Eye Movement Desensitization and Reprocessing) is another psychotherapeutic technique that brings healing to those suffering from PTSD (Post Traumatic Stress Disorder). Such individuals often experience angry outbursts, agitation, severe anxiety, self-destructive behaviors and self-isolation—all examples of unwanted urges that need transforming. EMDR uses a client's own rapid, rhythmic eye movements to dampen the power of emotionally charged memories arising from past traumatic events. Studies show that EMDR works better for adulthood traumas than those from childhood. Yoga is a better remedy for trauma suffered in childhood.[115]

Bioenergetic Psychotherapy helps free energetic blocks in your body, which were created in the past as a way to defend against the five wounds of terror, abandonment, humiliation, betrayal and rejection. These blocks or character structures are so ingrained that they can influence the shape of your body and make you think this is who you really are.

In his early work, Wilhelm Reich developed this therapy and it was further elaborated and developed by Alexander Lowen and John Pierrakos.[116] My book, *Hidden Treasure: How to Break Free of Five Patterns that Hide Your True Self,*[117] describes these five personality structures and offers ways to transform these traumatic wounds through a series of psychological, energetic and spiritual exercises. Knowing about these structures helps you let go of false self-perceptions and become aware of your True Nature (the Hidden Treasure).

Conclusion

Purification is a long, involved and difficult process whether it requires stripping away or transformation. I marvel at the many helpful techniques available to help you transform those energies that need redirecting. Some of these techniques such as meditation, prayer, breathing practices, chakras and yoga date back thousands of years. Some, such as Feeding Your Demons and the Forgiveness Prayer, are updates of earlier methods. Others, such as EMDR, pendulation, active imagination and bioenergetic therapy come from modern times. Thankfully, the use of transformation through mortification methods such as hair shirts or excessive fasting have mostly fallen into disuse. Modern psychological and spiritual techniques have replaced them and are just as effective, sometimes more so. Difficulties that arise from your past may cause considerable anguish. Sometimes you may wonder if you can take much more. During these times, you may find comfort in the poem, "Tired of Speaking Sweetly" by Sufi poet, Hafiz (1315–1390).

God wants to reach out and manhandle us,
Break all our teacup talk of God.

If you had the courage and
Could give the Beloved His choice, some nights,

He would just drag you around the room
By your hair,
Ripping from your grip all those toys in the world
That bring you no joy . . .

God wants to manhandle us,
Lock us inside of a tiny room with Himself
And practice His dropkick.

The Beloved sometimes wants
To do us a great favor;

Hold us upside down
And shake all the nonsense out.

But when we hear
He is in such a "playful drunken mood"
Most everyone I know
Quickly packs their bags and hightails it
Out of town.[118]

Some days, it feels like you're being dragged around the room by your hair or that all that you've previously known is being shaken out of you. Realizing that your challenges and hardships are part of an ongoing releasing and transforming process will hopefully help you cope when such situations arise.

Reflections on Transformation as Restoration and Regeneration

1. What methods have you developed to quiet your mind?

2. Do you tend to approach unwanted tendencies through willful submission or through acceptance and love?

3. You could experiment with the many transformative techniques available today and choose which ones are most effective for you.

4. If you have worked with some of the techniques described in this chapter, what were the results?

Chapter 8:
Clarifying Light–How Purification Happens in Your Everyday Life

One need not learn renunciation; life itself teaches it.

–HIK, *The Heart of Sufism*[119]

Both the releasing and transforming forms of purification are part of life. There's no escape. It shows up throughout your whole existence in different ways at different times. Sometimes, purification is active, as when you decide to release unproductive habits and improve your life. Other times, it's passive and unavoidable. Challenges, such as the death of a loved one, illness and aging, happen *to* you. When you see your difficulties through the lens of purification in particular and the spiritual journey in general, you might more easily understand—if not accept—why they came into your life. Giving your challenges and crises a name—"Ah, this is passive purification"—lessens their sting and clarifies the purpose to it all, namely, to further your spiritual growth. The most intense and frequent opportunities for purification usually occur in relationships, parenting, illness, aging and societal crises.

Relationships

Many of the faults you see in others, dear reader,
Are your own nature reflected in them.

–Rumi[120]

Deep, intimate relationships such as marriage, provide great opportunities for purification. The spiritual master Sai Baba (1926–2011) aptly described marriage as "the sandpapering of the ego."[121] Bumping up against a partner on a daily basis hopefully forces you to look at how you contribute to any disharmony in your relationship. You might decide to let go of or alter your negative behaviors as you relate to your partner, including any temptation to cast blame. You might need to relinquish some of your egoic desires and be sensitive to your partner's desires. For instance, you might have to postpone your own sexual desire if your partner is not interested or available at a particular time. During these times, you could redirect your energy upward as indicated in the fountain practice described in the previous chapter.

None of this is easy. The ego loves to be in control and win at all costs even if it disrupts the harmony between you and your loved one. I find myself always wanting to have the last word in a disagreement with my husband even when I know I need to let it go. I have such a driving need to be right.

The Audacity of Humility

I walked up to an old, old man and asked him.
"What is the audacity of humility?"
This man had never met me before,
but do you know what his answer was?
"To be the first to say, 'I love you.'"

–Theophane the Monk, *Tales of a Magic Monastery*[122]

I like to distinguish between self with a small "s" (your ego self) and Self with a big "S" (your soul). Healthy relationships help you purify your selfish (or egoic) desires but can go too far when they demand that you surrender your Selfish (or soul) desires. Your Selfish desires reflect the Divine flow working in you, which in turn positively affects your partner and everyone in your orbit, even though it may be difficult for them at first.

Recently, I counseled a couple struggling with their marriage. The wife had the idealized belief that being a good wife meant sacrificing her soul desires for those of her husband's. A good wife, she believed, was supposed to make dinner, wash and fold his clothes, clean the house and be available to her husband when he needed her. She abandoned her Self-ish or soul desires believing they were selfish. The best relationships are ones in which both partners make an effort to forego their selfish desires when necessary and honor their own and their partner's soul desires.

Noelle Poncelet, a psychotherapist and guide in the shamanic tra-dition, gives us a great example of both partners working together to celebrate each one's soul desires and still maintain harmony.

> My marriage is a twenty-four hour a day job. . . . I work all the time to be true to myself and to be honest with my husband. Not to give in early for the sake of compromise, but to wait, to listen, to find with him the creative solution that comes from putting our two energies together and tolerating the tension of conflict. It isn't easy to sustain our differences rather than watering them down, to let the momentum build until a new solution emerges. But it is exciting, and after thirty years of marriage, it's this kind of full-time engagement that lets the spirit of the relationship itself be a teacher for us.[123]

Purification often requires you to let go of expectations or ideal-ized notions about your relationships. You may become disillusioned because you have an idealized concept of what a relationship should be. You may put your partner on a pedestal only to be disappointed when he or she falls off. You may even need to release an idealized con-cept of yourself, as Jerry, a source quoted in *Hidden Treasure*, realized.

> I loved attracting women, especially when I played my guitar onstage. I'd project the image of having it all together because it made me feel alive and desired. I love the game, but no rela-tionship ever seemed to work out. In getting to know each other, we'd both become disillusioned. She was no longer attracted to me, and I saw that I was not the projected image I thought I was. Finally, I could no longer hide behind that false image.[124]

An acquaintance told me he had lived harmoniously with his partner for several years before they married, but after the wedding their relationship totally changed. Once they married, her expecta-tions of him altered dramatically because she had an idealized image of what a husband should be and do. He was supposed to take care of her and be more responsible around the house. Releasing any idealized version of ourselves or others is critical for inner growth and harmonious relationships.

Giving Birth—Parenting

Recently, I attended a Blessing Way—a beautiful ceremony for expectant mothers consisting of poetry, songs, words of support, laying on of hands and other rituals. Those who had children repeatedly gave the expectant mother the same advice: surrender to the process, to your body's wisdom, and let go of what you expect to happen during labor and birth. This is purification in action! Many mothers-to-be create a birthing plan, or they're confident they will be on top of the process. Such plans and attitudes often evaporate in the midst of the real event. Purification in this case involves stripping away any pride and control (or the illusion of control) and requires surrendering to what is.

Giving birth is only the beginning. Parenting provides many opportunities for purification, which makes it great training for the spiritual life. It constantly requires you to surrender to something greater than yourself—your child's welfare. You may be forced to let go of your attachment to sleep, plans, serenity, schedules or optimal job performance. This prepares you for the spiritual journey, which calls you to surrender your personal ego to the Divine flow, to the all-pervading Love of the Universe.

> A two-year old is kind of like having a blender,
> But you don't have a top for it.
> —Jerry Seinfeld[125]

Parenting stretches you and highlights your natural, but sometimes latent, unselfishness.

Illness

Purification intensifies even more when you become ill. It forces you to stop your usual activities and surrender to what's happening to you in the moment. Physically, illness requires you to relinquish feeling good or being free of pain. Psychologically, the failure of your body can affect your self-identity or self-image. Women in particular suffer from a change in their body-image because society puts such emphasis on how a woman looks. For instance, many women dread losing their hair during chemotherapy treatments, and men often fear their illness will affect their identity as a man.

Purification doesn't have to be this severe. I once developed a blocked oil gland on my eyelid (chalazion), which caused my eye to swell almost to closure. I needed an operation to unblock the duct, but they couldn't schedule it for a month. I taught my classes, shopped and interacted with others, all looking lopsided for a very long month. I tried wearing glasses, but my sons told me they didn't hide the deformity. This ordeal felt particularly hard because of my attachment to my self-image. I wish I could say this attachment is totally gone, but that's not the case. Society's standards on beauty are still deeply ingrained in my psyche.

Buddhist teachers like to make a distinction between pain or discomfort and suffering. Pain is a physical experience and part of the human condition. Suffering is created by the story you tell yourself about the pain. Your story could be saying, "God is punishing me," or "This happened because there's something wrong with me," or "This pain will never go away."

I find it easier to navigate pain if I adjust my stories to make room for a higher purpose. I might say, "My suffering is part of the purification process, which will lead me to something greater," or "I'm working off karma." These are still stories, but they place the pain in a different, more positive light. Ultimately, the goal is to give up all stories so as to not muddy the present moment, and totally accept and surrender to what an illness brings.

Aging

Purification becomes even more intense and frequent in later life. As you age, you often are forced to let go of your idealized physical image of good looks, strength, stamina or agility. Unless you have cosmetic surgery, you are likely to be greeted by wrinkles and sagging skin every time you look in the mirror. My Sufi guide told me she only sees light when looking in the mirror. That's something to emulate.

Later life often compels you to let go of your busyness and drive because you don't have the energy to keep up a fast pace. You may find yourself questioning your identity as a contributing member of society, especially if your identity has centered on what you do and produce rather than who you are. You may need to release other roles or identities, such as your identity as a parent, especially if your child is now "parenting" you, or as a professional, when you can no longer compete with younger colleagues at work.

Not wanting to face your decline, you may still cling to the same activities and social or family roles. As you age, you can easily fall into one of the dangers of the Dark Wood Stage as you frantically try to go back—or remain attached—to your old way of life that no longer suits. As a result, you might become bewildered or depressed, not realizing there's another quieter, deeper stage to life's journey—one of seeking liberation or enlightenment.

Aging often generates great fear. Signs of physical or mental decline often force a reckoning with the great unknown ahead. Questions arise, such as Will I get sick and suffer great pain? What will my death be like? How can I leave my loved ones? Purification in aging happens at a cellular level, preparing you for the ultimate letting go that comes with death. You can soften this fear by connecting with your True Nature, which never dies. Anandamayi Ma beautifully expresses what it's like to totally identify with her True Nature and live fully in the world but not be afraid of death. When Yogananda asked her about her life, she responded:

> Father, there is little to tell. . . . My consciousness has never associated itself with this temporary body. Before I came on this earth, Father, "I was the same." As a little girl, "I was the same." I grew into womanhood, but still "I was the same." When the family in which I had been born made arrangements to have this body married, "I was the same. . . ." And, Father, in front of you now, "I am the same." Ever afterward, though the dance of creation change[s] around me in the hall of eternity, "I shall be the same."[126]

During one retreat, spanning over the time of a milestone birthday, I struggled with the fear of aging, illness and death. The future looked bleak. Would I experience some dreadful illness, lose my mind, require a walker or have an oxygen tank dangling at my side? Would I sit around and watch TV all day long?

The morning of my birthday, with light streaming in my window, I woke up with Anandamayi Ma's words in my mind. Immediately, the fear dissipated, bringing me peace. Here was the solution to my fear. I could focus on the part of me that never changes and repeat, "I am the same whether I become ill, enfeebled or die." Saying these words brings me great comfort. I no longer think terrifying thoughts about the future. It will evolve in the way it's intended.

Hindu Four Stages of Life

While Western society tends to view aging negatively, the Hindu understanding of life stages puts aging in a more positive light. It postulates four stages that span the complete arc of human life. They are: (1) student, (2) householder, (3) retirement and (4) renunciation or liberation.[127] In the first stage, the student's primary duty is to learn. Although learning continues throughout life, the focus shifts to other responsibilities after the schooling years.

During the householder stage, you become an active member of society. Responsibilities of home, family, career and service to society prevail. Westerners and many modern Hindus get stuck in this stage, believing they'll be "over the hill" or lead a meaningless life if they move on. Advertising doesn't help. Even with graying hair, we are told, you need to be beautiful, energetic, athletic and totally engaged in activities more suited for younger folk. The Hindu model recognizes that there are potentially even more meaningful stages ahead and can transform aging into an attractive rather than dreaded stage of life's journey.

The third Hindu stage, retirement, begins sometime after the first grandchild is born or when the wrinkles and gray hair appear. Hindus see this stage as a time to let go of outer responsibilities and busyness in order to focus on inner spiritual development. It's a time to read, meditate, attend spiritual retreats and seek answers to the larger questions.[128]

Granted, people in our society today often plan their retirement in interesting ways—travel, gardening, study, socializing, but the Hindu third stage takes retirement to a deeper level.

During the fourth or renunciation stage, seekers have reached the goal of the spiritual life. They have released all self-identities to now see life from the consciousness of the whole. They are at home everywhere—in the busyness of the marketplace or the quiet of nature, with others or alone. No longer overly attached to people or things, the liberated ones are ready to accept whatever comes their way, such as moving into an assisted living facility or struggling with a serious illness, because they are now connected to the eternal part of themselves, and this fosters an inner serenity. Just their presence uplifts all who come in contact with them—an ideal to which we can all aspire.

Growth Follows Purification

At each stage of life, purification ushers in personal growth. Being in a close relationship or parenting a child helps you experience profound love. You realize that true love is stronger than personal desire. Because you love, you become willing to give up your ego attachments for the one you love whether that person is your partner, your child or a dear friend. For many mystics, the love for the Divine is so great that they become willing to undergo great sacrifices.

In a Tree House

Love will certainly bust you wide open
Into an unfettered, blooming new galaxy
Even if your mind is a spoiled mule.
A life-giving radiance will come,
The Friend's gratuity will come.

–Hafiz, *The Subject Tonight is Love*[129]

Illness and societal crises compel you to re-examine your life and its purpose. What you had thought was so important may no longer be so. You may realize that you are not in control of your life. These considerations may turn you toward or renew your commitment to the Radiant All. You may also discover previously unknown qualities arising within you such as courage, compassion or creativity.

As an elder, you might experience spiritual gifts more often because there's more psychological space for you to receive them.[130] You now have more time to meditate, attend retreats, read about spiritual subjects and ask the deeper questions about life. As the Hindu schemata attests, you might realize that this time of life is an opportunity to embrace a new direction, a new stage of life—one even more important than the previous life stages.

Societal Purification: Pandemics and Wars

Periodically, purification happens to society as a whole in the form of wars or pandemics. Perhaps life has become so out of balance that a major correction is needed. Examples of today's society gone askew are the drastically changing climate, the widening split between rich and poor or between people of color and whites, and the strong cultural and social pressures to succeed no matter what its cost to others.

Wars and pandemics can purify your sense of being the director of your own world. How can you feel secure and in control when bombs are exploding, or you are forced to confront the reality that you could get sick and die at any moment? Facing imminent death can strip away your egoic desires for status, wealth, fine clothes, possessions, power, self-importance or even wanting things to go your way. Suddenly, your anger at another person or situation pales in comparison to the thought of your death. You're forced to realize that what you thought was important may not be so. All these situations foster purification, like it or not.

Purification transforms. Societal crises produce courage, heroism, compassion and creativity. Wars and pandemics usher in societal growth and major shifts in consciousness. There are many examples from Western history. The Black Death caused the populace to question the authority of the Church because it was unable to avert the disaster. This opened the way for the Protestant Reformation. WWI and the 1918 Spanish Flu dismantled the class system in Europe, led to the collapse of four empires,[131] and provided the last impetus for women to win the right to vote.

The wake of WWII ushered in a great change in American lifestyle. The middle class grew, thanks to a great economic boom, and the acceleration in technology created a better quality of life. The US became more involved in European affairs and asserted its role as a superpower.

Overall, wars and pandemics initiate growth and awareness. I don't know why such extreme purification and its attendant acute suffering is needed to clear the way for change in societal consciousness. Perhaps it's comparable to the pain of childbirth, which is a necessary part of bringing a glorious new life into the world.

Conclusion

You don't have to look for ways to navigate the purification stage of the journey. Life amply presents that opportunity. It's a slow, difficult process, but seeing your life through the lens of purification and its ensuing growth clarifies its purpose and helps you to better accept its sting. You may even come to understand and experience the Love behind these challenges, inviting you to a greater, more fulfilling life.

Reflections on Purification in Everyday Life

1. How can you maintain a balance between giving to others and remaining true to yourself?

2. What needs purifying in your relationships? Have you learned to be yourself in your relationships rather than to live up to an idealized version of who you think you should be?

3. Are you able to separate your pain from your stories about your pain?

4. You may want to tune into that part of you—your True Nature— that feels no sickness, pain or bodily decline. Such a practice helps you become more conscious of the Divine within you.

5. Where has purification appeared in the various stages of your life?

Chapter 9:
Ever-Increasing Light–Illumination

The brain speaks through words;
The heart in the glance of the eyes;
And the soul through a radiance that charges the atmosphere,
Magnetizing all.[132]

–HIK, *The Complete Sayings*

The glorious experiences of the Illumination Stage serve as a welcome relief from the purification process. Whether active or passive, purification is not easy. Attachments are stripped away or given up. Painful traumas surface that require healing. Ideas you hold dear are smashed.

Happily, these difficulties take a rest during the Illumination Stage. You may find that your creativity, compassion, insight and intuition increase and your connection with nature deepens. Your spiritual senses might open, enabling you to witness visions of light, hear celestial music, taste a sweet nectar and smell an indescribable perfume.

The Illumination Stage is similar to the Awakening Stage (as discussed in Chapter 4), because it also involves a direct experience of the Radiant All. However, Illumination lasts longer, appears more frequently and expands your range of experiences.

Illumination brings you more certainty about the existence of the Radiant All, whether you experience it deep within or beyond you. This gives you a new vitality, comfort and peace. You have more strength to continue the journey during times of discouragement and difficulty. More and more, you may experience a permeating presence, whether you engage in prayer and meditation or undertake the tasks of daily life. St. Teresa of Ávila (1512-1582) declared she had found her God easily among the pots and pans.[133] I often think of this when doing the dishes. At least I become more mindful of my actions, if not enlightened. Even when the pendulum swings back to the Purification Stage and you no longer directly experience the divine presence, you never forget its existence.

Inevitably, the glorious experiences of the Illumination begin to fade or disappear. You may be tempted to hold on to these experiences but unavoidably fail. Adyashanti uses the metaphor of a rocket taking off. If it doesn't have enough energy to break through the gravitational field and continue on, it falls back down to earth. This means the seeker returns again to an egoic state of consciousness.[134] What a disappointment! "Oh, no," you might say. "Here I am back again in my ordinary state of consciousness when I thought I'd left it behind. I thought I'd reached the final goal."

This oscillation between the illuminative experiences of your True Nature and your egoic self continues, but gradually, more and more time is spent in the Illumination Stage. John of the Cross in *Living Flame of Love* explains it well.

> In this state, the soul is like the crystal that is clear and pure, the more degrees of light it receives, the greater concentration of light that there is in it . . . [until it appears] to be wholly light and cannot be distinguished from the light.[135]

Exalted as this may be, it's still not the final resting place. More growth is required. You still need to travel some rocky roads before reaching the final, Unitive Stage—final awakening—when the rocket leaves the gravitational field and there's no return to egoic consciousness. It takes courage and determination to continue on the path without running away.

The Divine as Beloved

The illuminated state may take the form of a deep love relationship between the seeker and the Divine. Christian wisdom calls this state of dual consciousness the Betrothal or Engagement, and it precedes the final state of unity, titled Marriage. One of the Hindu paths, Bhakti yoga, focuses on loving devotion to a personal God. Unlike other Hindu sects that aim at total union with the Divine, devotees of Bhakti yoga would rather stay in a state of Divine-as-other, claiming "I want to taste sugar, not be sugar."[136]

A relationship with the Beloved involves communication as true for any relationship. It may take the form of seeking and receiving answers from the Beloved, or offering gratitude, devotion and praise to this Holy Love. Sometimes this communication takes the shape of an inner dialogue. Other times, you may simply sense a higher presence or energy, which at times courses through your body, opening up the chakras or energy centers, causing you to give thanks for this delicious experience.

Examples of the relationship between the seeker and the Divine appear in many spiritual traditions:

- Sufis address the Divine as Beloved. "Enter unhesitatingly, Beloved, for in this abode there is naught but yearning for Thee."[137]

- The *Song of Songs* in the Hebrew Bible sensually expresses the relationship between lover and Beloved. "Let him kiss me with the kisses of his mouth. Your love is more delightful than wine." (1:1)[138]

- The Book of Proverbs gives a less voluptuous illustration of a loving dialogue. "I love those who love me; those who seek me eagerly shall find me." (8:17)[139]

- A strong relationship between Christians and Jesus appears in the New Testament and in later Christian writings. Jesus claims, "As the father has loved me, so I have loved you. Remain in my love." (John 15:9)[140]

- Songs of praise and devotion comprise the lexicon of Bhakti yoga. In this path, the devotee only needs to love God for no ulterior reason but for Love's sake alone.[141]

- The Hindu Bhagavad Gita contains a full-length dialogue between Krishna, an incarnation of the god Vishnu, and the warrior Arjuna. "Not by the Vedas [scriptures], or austere life, or gifts to the poor, or ritual offerings can I be seen as you have seen me. Only by love [bhakti] can people see me and know me and come unto me." (11:53–4)[142]

After a while, you might find your relationship with the Divine surpasses all other relationships, worthy as those may be. The feelings of expansion, energy and joy that you experience when first entering a romantic love fade over time but increase when loving the Divine. In describing her mystical experience of rebirth, Elisabeth Kübler-Ross says: "It was so incredibly beautiful that if I would describe it as a thousand orgasms at one time, it would be a very shabby comparison."[143] No wonder people join monasteries!

Mismatched Newlyweds

Like
a pair
of mismatched newlyweds,
one of whom still feels very insecure,
I keep turning to God
saying,
"Kiss
me."[144]

–Hafiz, *The Gift*

Sixth Oxherding Picture:
Riding the Ox Home

The Zen tradition doesn't recognize a personal god and has no examples of the relationship between the seeker and the Divine like the ones cited above. However, it acknowledges a dual consciousness between the seeker and Buddha mind (the Ox) as a preliminary step to final enlightenment.

The first six Oxherding pictures indicate this duality. At first, you can't even find the Ox (Dark Wood), although at some level it is always there. You then see the tracks (Finding the Way), followed by an actual glimpse of the Ox (Awakening). You understand the need to capture and tame the Ox (Purification) until it is so obedient that you can ride the Ox home (Illumination). Sitting on top of the Ox, the rider is connected to—yet still separate from—the Ox. Here is the commentary:

> The struggle is over, "gain" and "loss" no longer affect him. He hums the rustic tune of the woodsman and plays the simple songs of the village children. Astride the Ox's back, he gazes serenely at the clouds above. His head does not turn [in the directions of temptations]. Try though one may to upset him, he remains undisturbed.[145]

This passage highlights the happiness and serenity experienced during the Illumination Stage. The seeker is no longer tempted by un-manageable habits and unhealthy tendencies, free from anxieties and fear. Imagine what a relief this would be. Humming tunes and playing songs indicate the enhanced creativity that this stage brings. For the present, life is good.

Seventh Oxherding Picture:
Self Alone, Ox Forgotten

The seventh picture indicates the seeker's realization that he's no longer separated from the Ox. He *is* the Ox. There comes a time in spiritual development when the seeker realizes, as the Chandogya Upanishad claims, "Thou art That."[146] At that moment there is no duality, only moments of oneness. You don't need a practice during these times because you're already there, as the commentary states. "A trap is no longer needed when the rabbit has been caught, a net becomes useless when a fish has been snared."[147] These experiences of oneness fall short of the unitive or final awakening stage because they are not permanent—they come and go.

The Divine in Nature

Illumination may come in the form of awareness of the Radiant All encountered in nature. Perhaps when walking, you suddenly experience an aliveness permeating the trees, plants, lakes and rivers, and realize that the same life force pulsates through you and all things. Byron, a source for my doctoral thesis research, expresses it well:

> Then I experienced the world of life—the infinite variety of living cells—the vast expanse of the night skies with millions of stars, the sands and the sea. I felt the tree of life—the cosmic tree—growing up from the center of the earth . . . I saw my home—all the plants and trees, my children and my wife and the nuns at the nearby monastery. All formed a vast symphony of life.[148]

In looking at a hyacinth, Kathleen Raine (1908-2003) experienced the Divine flowing through it. "I was not perceiving the flower but living it. I was aware of the life of the plant as a slow flow or circulation of a vital current of liquid light of the utmost purity."[149]

The Christian mystic, Meister Eckhart, makes a similar point. "If I spent enough time with the tiniest creatures—even a caterpillar—I would never have to prepare a sermon. So full of God is every creature."[150]

As you are a part of nature, you might also experience this life force streaming through you. Viewing a sunset or engaging in the ordinary tasks of life, may transport you into a greater awareness of the Infinite in the present moment, as the famous Buddhist phrase exclaims.

> How wondrous this, how mysterious!
> I carry fuel, I draw water.[151]

Many poets, artists and musicians are inspired by an awareness of the Divine in nature. Examples include William Blake, Claude Monet and Claude Debussy. In *The Ten Sufi Thoughts*, HIK proclaims: "There is one Holy Book, the sacred manuscript Nature, the only scripture which can enlighten the reader."[152] St. Bernard of Clairvaux (1090-

1153) expresses the same sentiment: "What I know of the divine sciences and the holy scriptures, I learned in the woods and fields. I have no other masters other than the beeches and oaks."[153] Annie Dillard's famous *Pilgrim at Tinker Creek* connects with the Divine through her meditations on the fields, woods and mountains of Roanoke, VA.[154]

Advanced mystics connect so intimately with Nature that they are able to commune with ferocious animals and tame them. Legend has it that St. Francis changed the wolf who bothered the people of Assisi into a peaceful animal beloved by all. According to the Hebrew scriptures, Daniel survived a night in the den of hungry lions because of his harmony with the Divine.[155] It is said that when Hoyu-zenji practiced zazen, birds would offer him flowers as he sat in his hut.[156] St. Rose of Lima (1586–1617) also connected with birds in a musical duet.

> Each evening at sunset, a little bird with an enchanting voice came and perched upon a tree beside her window and waited until she gave the sign to him to sing. Rose, as soon as she saw her little feathered chorister, made herself ready to sing the praises of God, and challenged the bird to a musical duel in a song which she had composed for this purpose. "Begin, dear little bird," she said, "begin thy lovely song! . . ." At once the little bird began to sing, running through his scale to the highest note. Then he ceased, that the saint might sing in her turn . . . thus did they celebrate the greatness of God, turn by turn for a whole hour.[157]

Established in the 1960s, the Findhorn community exemplifies a different form of communication with creation. The founders interacted with nature spirits and devas (celestial beings), who told them how to develop a garden on the inhospitable sandy shores of northern Scotland. The devas told them where and when to plant and mulch each species. The nature spirits built up the energies or etheric counterparts of each plant.

Horticulturists couldn't figure out how such large vegetables (for example, forty-pound cabbages) and beautiful flowers of every variety could grow under such conditions.[158] Roc Crombie, a famous mathematician and a member of the Findhorn community, described these nature spirits and devas as intelligent whirls of colored lights who take on the form created by the myths and legends of human culture. Depending on their cultural background, individuals might envision these vortexes of lights as fairies, gnomes, devas or nature spirits. I always wondered about the existence of fairies and gnomes. Crombie's explanation makes the possibility of their reality more believable.[159]

Experiences of Light

In the Illumination Stage, you may experience ever-increasing, all-pervading light. These uplifting experiences of light appear in many spiritual traditions. Here are some examples:

- "The true light that enlightens everyone was coming into the world." John 1:9[160]

- "O splendor of God Eternal through which I saw the supreme triumph of the one true kingdom. Grant me the power to speak forth what I saw." Dante[161]

- "Some see Buddha's oceans of clouds of light, issuing from his pores, of radiant hues."[162]

- "There is a light within every soul; it only needs the clouds that overshadow it to be broken for it to beam forth." HIK[163]

- "If a thousand suns were to rise in the heavens at the same time, the blaze of their light would resemble the splendor of that Supreme Spirit." *The Bhagavad Gita*, 11:12[164]

Can you imagine a thousand suns in the sky? One sun on a cloudless day is bright enough. It boggles the mind. All these traditions seem to describe a similar reality.

After years of spiritual work and a sudden kundalini experience, Vijali Hamilton, a contemporary American woman, experienced this realm of light not as beyond but within all life.

I saw only light patterns and there were no boundaries or borders. It was as if my mind had once long ago made up a story about separate objects with boundaries, but the story wasn't true. The true story is that there is a luminous, spacious energy that flows through everything all the time. It's within matter, within things as well as within space, and you can tune in to it at any time, just like changing the frequency on the radio. There is no distance between this essence and ourselves. It is not other-worldly. It is right here, closer than our own flesh.[165]

Mystical experiences of light can occur spontaneously to individuals without any spiritual orientation or practice. In his article, "Visionary Experience," Aldous Huxley offers one such example.

I was a girl of 15 or 16. I was in the kitchen toasting bread for tea and suddenly on a dark November afternoon, the whole place was flooded with light, and for a minute by clock time, I was immersed in this, and I had a sense that in some unutterable way, the universe was all right. This has affected me the rest of my life, I have lost all fear of death, I have a passion for life, but I am in no way afraid of death, because this light experience has been a kind of conviction to me that everything is all right in some way.[166]

This passage demonstrates that experiences of light can occur at any time and any place. The young girl's encounter with light permanently changed her, which indicates a depth and authenticity to her experience.

In the same article, Huxley asks the intriguing question, "Why are precious stones precious?"[167] Why do we enjoy watching a fire, seeing a sunset or witnessing fireworks? His answer is simple. They remind us of this realm of light witnessed by those dwelling in the illuminative stage. To me, this means that some deep part of you remembers this light, that some deep part of you *is* light. It's a matter of accessing it, perhaps by concentrating on light or engaging in practices of light.

Encounters with light appear in the accounts of those undergoing a near death experience. According to Raymond Moody in *Life After Life*, of all the experiences a dying person may have, the most profound is an encounter with a very bright light. Often this light is described as a being of light who pours love, warmth and acceptance to the dying person.[168]

Some mystics attribute water and fire qualities to this primordial light. Mechthild of Magdeburg in her *Revelations* refers to the "Flowing Fire and Light of God."[169] Dante exclaims, "And I saw light that was a river flowing."[170] Byron, whose account of his experience is included in my dissertation thesis, describes this light as a "strangely bubbling light." It had "the quality of effervescence that we associate with water, a spring, fountain or waterfall."[171]

Such passages indicate that this light is different from the light of the sun. It has distinct qualities of water, fire and unsurpassed brightness. These inspiring passages are clearly better—although approximate—descriptions of the Divine than what passes for most people's understanding today.

Such experiences of light are often so powerful that you might think you've attained enlightenment or believe the light itself is God. Instead, they indicate you are progressing on the path, but not yet there. In truth, the Divine Essence cannot be articulated as light or anything else. The apophatic Christian mystics, such as Meister Eckhart, acknowledged that God has no image.[172] The Flemish mystic Ruysbroeck (1293–1381) described the illuminated state as not God but "the Light in which we see" God.[173] Another way to rephrase this teaching is to say the Radiant God includes, but is even beyond, light.

Light Radiating from a Person

My Brilliant Image

I wish I could show you,
when you are lonely and in darkness
the Astonishing Light
of your own Being

–Hafiz, *I Heard God Laughing*[174]

Another form of light experience consists of seeing light radiating from a person. Some mystics can be so immersed in light that others can actually see it. Both the Hebrew and Christian scriptures give similar accounts of this phenomenon. "When Moses came down from Mt. Sinai, with the two tablets of testimony in his hand . . . the skin of his face shone because he had been talking with God."[175] Three of the apostles witnessed light emanating from Jesus, whose "face shone like the sun and his garments became white as light."[176]

The most vivid account I've found of light radiating from a person is that of a disciple of Saint Seraphim of Sarov (1754–1833) of the Russian Orthodox Church. His initial experience of his master radiating light was so strong that he couldn't look at him. "I can't look at you, Father, your eyes flash lightning, your face is more dazzling than the sun, and it hurts my eyes to look at you."[177] After Seraphim began to pray, the disciple discovered he was able to look at him.

> I looked and was seized with pious fear. Imagine the face of a man speaking to you from the middle of the sun, from the brightness of its dazzling midday beams. You see his lips moving, the changing expression in his eyes, you hear his voice, you feel his hands holding you by the shoulders, but you do not see those hands or the body of the man who is speaking to you, nothing but the shining light that spreads for many yards around him, revealing with its beams the snow-covered field outside and the white flakes that steadily go on falling.[178]

I'm blown away each time I read this passage. Not only does it confirm the earlier Biblical accounts that such experiences are possible, but it graphically makes you a witness to the disciple's experience.

You don't have to reach these high states of consciousness to radiate light. I often perceive this radiance emanating—to a lesser extent—from someone who has completed a seven day or longer retreat. Perhaps you also sense light in certain individuals you've encountered throughout your life.

In addition to sensing the presence of the Divine in nature and witnessing dazzling light on its own or emanating from a person, the illuminative state enhances the creative, intuitive, intellectual and emotional aspects of your being. It may also heighten your spiritual senses. What are these phenomena? The following chapter delves into such experiences and offers some answers.

Reflections on Illumination

1. Have you experienced light or energy, or something invisible, within nature? Has your heart been opened when viewing nature?

2. Have you ever observed someone whose face seems to radiate light?

3. You might want to work with practices of light:

    a. Breathe in light. Breathe out light several times. Feel light fill you. You don't have to actually "see" light but can simply "sense" it

    b. Say repeatedly, with eyes opened or closed: "My body, heart and soul radiate divine light" and imagine light extending beyond you to your surroundings.

    c. Imagine light in each of your chakras.

    d. Connect with a sense of your inner light when watching a sunset or gazing at a fire.

Chapter 10:
Exalted Light–Illumination and Heightened Awareness

Even as bright and shining objects, once touched by a ray of light falling on them, become even more glorious and themselves cast another light, so too souls that carry the Spirit and are enlightened by the Spirit, become spiritual themselves and send forth grace upon others. This grace enables them to foresee the future, to understand mysteries, to grasp hidden things, to receive spiritual blessings, to have their thoughts fixed on spiritual (heavenly) things, to dance with the angels. So is their joy unending, so is their perseverance in God unfailing, so do they acquire likeness to God, so—most sublime of all—do they themselves become divine.

–St. Basil, the Great (330–379)[179]

This quotation dramatically tells of the many gifts that occur most often during the Illumination Stage. This pouring forth of the Divine in you can deepen, broaden or intensify your emotional experience and creative impulses. It can heighten your awareness, enhance your intuitive abilities, and expand your understanding of the world. Your spiritual senses may also develop during the Illumination Stage. You may see, hear, touch, taste and smell invisible worlds, experiencing and understanding other realms in new ways. Sometimes paranormal powers develop. While all these experiences may bring you closer to the ultimate goal of the spiritual journey, they are not the goal themselves.

Heightened Compassion, Creativity, Intuition and Understanding

Heightened Compassion

Your emotions become deeper and more expansive during these heightened states of awareness. You may be less emotionally reactive to life's challenges and experience deeper states of peace. Feelings of joy and gratitude may be so expanded that you find yourself increasingly weeping as you take in the beauty of the natural world. You may also find yourself laughing more often because you don't take yourself so seriously or worry so much about the vicissitudes of daily life.

Two Giant Fat People

God
And I have become
Like two giant fat people
Living in a Tiny boat.
We
Keep
L-a-u-g-h-i-n-g.

–Hafiz, *The Gift*[180]

You may experience a greater sensitivity to and empathy for others and the suffering of the planet. HIK would express a deep sadness when he perceived suffering in the world. He had to interrupt a lecture once in 1923 because he sensed a terrible catastrophe and callings for help in the Far East. The next day, the newspapers published accounts of the great earthquake in Japan.[181] This sensitivity to the world's suffering is balanced by a deep understanding that beneath all worldly happenings lies love and peace.

Heightened Creativity

You may experience a flowering of your creativity resulting in an out-pouring of poetry, music, writing or painting. This may differ from other creative bursts you've experienced, which might involve more effort. When this flow occurs, artists, poets and musicians admit they can't take credit for these works. Rather, they claim these creations had poured through them as though they were vessels for something greater.

Have you experienced this delicious sense of something beyond your conscious mind acting through you? Perhaps you played a musical piece perfectly up until the time you became conscious of how well you were doing and then made a mistake. Maybe you experienced being "in the flow" when playing a sport. Without any effort, you played the game perfectly because you felt something greater acting through you.

Examples of enhanced creativity flowing through a master appear throughout history. The German abbess, Hildegaard of Bingen claimed to have received no education in music, yet she wrote beautifully soaring chants of devotion still enjoyed today. Her creativity was plentiful in many areas including poetry, art and mystical writings. Legend claims that Lao Tzu took three days to compose the exquisite and inspiring *Tao Te Ching* after a border guard asked him to record his wisdom before leaving China.[182] Handel wrote *The Messiah* in twenty-four days. Convent rules only allowed Teresa of Ávila to write for one hour each day, so without rereading what she had previously written—even if she had stopped in the middle of a sentence—she began where she had left off. In this way, she wrote her famous *Interior Castle,* considered to be one of the most profound of all mystical writings.

Heightened Intuition/Understanding

You may notice an increase in your intuition at this time. You may gain greater insights and understanding of events in your everyday life, such as how to navigate a thorny situation. You may gain knowledge of the workings of the cosmos and see how all things work together for the benefit of all.

The Protestant mystic Jacob Boehme (1575–1624), a shoe cobbler with little education, came to a profound understanding of the origin of the cosmos during a state of illumination: "In this earnest seeking, the Gate was opened to me, that in one Quarter of an Hour [sic] I saw and I knew more than if I had been many years at a university."[183]

Boehme saw the Divine essence, the creation of life, and the three worlds—divine, angelic and material—and how they fit together. He saw the origin and essence of good and evil. Profound insights came to him—all in fifteen minutes.

My own experience of heightened understanding and clarity happened during a silent group retreat. I sat in the back of the dining room looking at the others, all of whom were quietly eating, absorbed in their own state of inner awareness. Suddenly the scene shifted into a different dimension. I saw each come out of a form and then back into it, like a wave ebbing and flowing. I saw how everyone present was designed to come together in that moment in time and it was perfect.

Such experiences of expanded knowledge appear in the accounts of individuals after they were declared clinically dead for up to two hours. As Raymond Moody notes in his *Reflections on Life after Life*, some individuals experience a vision of all knowledge.[184] However, the subjects claimed they could not bring this knowledge back with them when they returned to their bodies. The following account from Moody's book is similar to Boehme's experience.

> This seemed to take place after I had seen my life pass before me. It seemed that all of a sudden, all knowledge—of all that had started from the very beginning, that would go on without end—that for a second I knew all the secrets of all ages, all the meaning of the universe, the stars, the moon—of everything.[185]

These accounts are not only enticing, but also remind me of the Akashic records—a term posited by theosophy and anthroposophy and purportedly a non-physical, etheric realm, consisting of all human events, past, present and future. Do individuals in the Illumination Stage tap into the same states of consciousness as those declared clinically dead? Are they experiencing the Akashic records?

The Spiritual Senses

During the Illumination Stage, you may experience heightened sensory awareness beyond the physical plane. You may experience a higher, non-physical octave of sight, sound, touch, taste and smell. In mystical literature these are called the spiritual senses. Your primary orientation (visual, auditory or kinesthetic) might influence what kind of heightened sensory experience you may have. Or have first. For instance, if your orientation is primarily auditory, you may first hear other-worldly sounds; if visual, then you might see images or visions. Most likely you will not experience the heightening of all the spiritual senses, but certainly some of them. What is the meaning of these experiences? Should you pay attention to them? I would like to explore these heightened sensory experiences first before considering their meaning and authenticity.

Visions

As recounted in the last chapter, many mystical experiences have a visual component. Visions may include experiences of formless light, a person radiating light, or light permeating the natural world. These visions can also take a prophetic form such as revealed in the Book of Revelation and the writings of Nostradamus. In several visions, Hildegaard of Bingen predicted the fall of the Holy Roman Empire and the Protestant Reformation, centuries before they occurred. She also had visions of the "higher spheres," which one of her nuns beautifully illustrated.[186]

Teresa of Ávila distinguishes between three types of visions: corporeal, imaginal and intellectual.[187] Corporal or bodily visions are similar to hallucinations. They appear outside of you. Unlike corporeal visions, imaginal visions appear to your inner eye. You can't mistake them for anything tangible. Intellectual visions can hardly be classed as visions at all because they have no internal or external sensory component. Rather, they are a radical, formless imprinting on your mind, an inner knowing that never fades with time. Teresa claims the chance for deception decreases with intellectual visions, because there's less chance for your own psychological material to interfere. They're not ultimate truth, but they hold some validity.

Auditions

You might experience a heightened sense of sound, which may first appear as a buzzing, chime or bell. Eventually, you may hear beautiful, celestial music. Hearing such music often transports you into a state of happiness and peace. As John of the Cross reveals, "The soul feels a spiritual voice and noise which is above all sounds and voices. . . . This voice is accompanied by grandeur, strength, power, delights and glory."[188] Heightened hearing may come in the form of a dialogue with a higher being. Christian mystical literature abounds with this type of hearing.[189]

Channeling, popular in the 1970s, can also be a form of heightened auditory experience. The channeler conveys to the audience the words they hear from other dimensions, which may range from the channeler's own flawed unconscious material to some high level of consciousness.[190] At one time my husband served as a spiritualist minister. To my surprise and awe, he gave inspiring twenty-minute sermons without any previous preparation. Wondering where these sermons came from, I asked him about his experience.

"I'd pray and open myself up. I'd feel like I'm standing in a stream, allowing the teaching to flow through me. I just needed to keep the channel open and not interfere," he said.

Enhanced Touch, Taste and Smell

In addition to visions and auditions, you may experience a heightened sense of touch coming from a place beyond the physical realm. While practicing energy work in my classes, some students receiving healing energy would sense the practitioner's hands still on their body minutes after they had been removed. This could be explained by a physical reaction to the energy received in the treatment, although it generally occurs on only one part of the body. It's a little more difficult to explain Fr. John's experience during his time at the Thomas Merton Center for Contemplative Prayer. He told me about one day while alone in his room and lying on his bed, he recalled a shameful incident from his past and exclaimed, "I really need a good kick in the pants!" Suddenly he felt a strong kick in his rear, which to his surprise sent him flying in the air, landing him on the floor beside his bed.

The heightened sense of taste often appears as sweet nectar, which some mystical traditions explain as hormonal secretions of the pineal gland. This happens most often during deep meditation practice. A heightened sense of smell can reflect the presence of positive or negative energy. St. Thérèse of Lisieux's presence is often associated with the smell of roses. A person can also sense a putrid sulfur-like smell when encountering strong negativity.

Christmas at the Monastery

For Christmas why don't you go to the Magic Monastery? . . . The three Wise Men are there also. Each Christmas one of them will give the sermon. Listen very carefully. You may have difficulty with his language, but that is because he is so wise and you are foolish. I thought he was superficial, talking about incense on Christmas. It was only later that I realized he had been talking about the REAL incense, and now I can smell that wherever I go. Perhaps when you go there, he will be speaking about the real gold, or the real myrrh.
And then there are the angels. You'll hear them singing. What shall I say? It's God's music. It gets into your bones. Nothing is the same afterwards.
But all this is nothing. What really matters is when the Word becomes flesh. Wait till you experience that.

–Theophane the Monk, *Tales of the Magic Monastery*[191]

These enhanced spiritual senses can arise during heightened experiences of ordinary people. I recently read about a lawyer who was an active alcoholic throughout his education and two marriages. Wanting to become sober, he tried AA but couldn't accept the second step—recognizing that a Higher Power could help conquer his addiction. "I thought all the spiritual stuff was a bunch of starched, hypocritical baloney," he said. A week into sobriety, he was overcome by a strong desire to drink. His sponsor told him to eat chocolate (I love this!), take a bath, and get on his knees, asking God for help. The first two directives initially helped, but the craving returned in full force. He reluctantly decided to follow the third suggestion to pray for help.

Ducking beneath the apartment window, where people might see me, I knelt and lowered my head to the rug. I felt like a fool. "Please help me," I mumbled. A wave of peace washed over me. All the fears and insecurities I'd spent years dousing with alcohol vanished. Deep in my soul, I knew that somehow everything in my chaotic life would turn out okay. My body went limp with relief. I opened my eyes to crawl toward my futon. The room was permeated by a warm, white light, which seemed to come from everywhere and nowhere. I pulled myself onto the futon and lay down. A gentle hand stroked my back. Under any other circumstance, that experience would have freaked me out. I just lay there, feeling loved and held. Thirty years later, I still tear up thinking about it.[192]

In this account, a non-believer experienced several of the increased human capabilities and heightened senses: deep peace (emotion), permeating light (sight), a gentle hand stroking his back (touch), and the inner sense that everything would be okay (knowing).

Energetic Effects

A tremendous increase of energy often can accompany these heightened states of awareness. Blocks in the body can be released either subtly or dramatically and this can affect the nervous system. Adyashanti claims the wiring of the mind can be undone and redone differently to produce more clarity.[193] You might have trouble sleeping because so much energy is coursing through your body, or you might find your heart racing or feel your body jerking (called kriyas in the Hindu tradition). The heightened state of awareness can also make you more sensitive to your environment and to other people's energies. Hindus developed systems such as Hatha and Kriya yoga to help strengthen the body so it could withstand and process this increase in energy.

Development of Paranormal Powers

During the Illumination Stage, you may develop paranormal powers, called *siddhis* in the Hindu tradition. These include out-of-body experiences, bilocation (being in two places at the same time), healing abilities, a discerning of others' hearts, sensing atmospheres, creating material objects out of nothing, and sensing the future.

The late Sathya Sai Baba is said to have repeatedly materialized *vibhuti* (ash) and small material objects out of nothing. He'd make a circular motion with an open, empty hand and bring his fingers together to produce a created object.[194] He believed modern people would reject other-worldly dimensions unless they saw something with their own eyes. This was the rationale behind his actions. Sai Baba married two of my friends. During the ceremony he circled his arm with opened hand, then closed his hand, during which they heard a clinking noise. When he opened his hand, they witnessed to their surprise two rings lying there with exactly the right sizes. Hearing this story, I wondered if the story of Jesus' multiplication of the loaves and fishes has a basis in reality (John 6:1-15).[195]

Padre Pio (1887–1968), a Capuchin friar and priest, was known to both bilocate and levitate. He would be seen walking in the village and simultaneously celebrating Mass elsewhere. Attendees would also see him levitate while saying Mass.[196] According to historical accounts, Thomas Aquinas (1225–1274)[197] and other mystics also levitated. Certain members of the present-day Transcendental Meditation (TM) community purportedly levitate. Sprinkled throughout his book, *Autobiography of a Yogi*, Yogananda gives accounts of the various yogic powers demonstrated by the individuals he meets.[198] Super-normal powers are also experienced by Buddhist practitioners after they achieve a certain degree of realization. Nagarjuna claims that these are not just attained by Buddhists but others who have seriously developed their spiritual life.[199] Such powers include walking on water, traveling through walls, becoming invisible, and bilocation. Following his enlightenment, Buddha himself was said to possess many of these powers.[200] I marvel at these individuals with such psychic powers in the same way that I admire Olympic athletes for their bodily feats, but know I'll never possess them. Luckily, they are not essential for spiritual development.

Early in my spiritual development, I foolishly concentrated on developing out-of-body experiences. Once during this state, I saw many thick, coarse arms and hands reaching toward me from each side, wanting me to come their way. I then heard the celestial music found in a schmaltzy religious film and saw a beautifully refined hand coming down from way above me. I said I want to go *there*, and at that moment the crass hands disappeared. This showed me that I needed to concentrate on higher spiritual aspirations, not psychic phenomenon.

Meaning and Authenticity Questions

The authenticity of these types of expanded awareness, sensory experiences, and supernatural powers has been questioned throughout history. Are they hallucinations, auto-suggestions, disturbed psychological activity, or do they reflect a real higher level of consciousness? Not one answer suffices. Some of the accounts are most likely authentic, reflecting the intermediary realms of consciousness, some are mixed with the individuals' psychological material, and others are some type of psychological or pathological aberration. Clearing away as much of your psychological issues as possible during the purification process and deepening your meditative practice reduces psychological interference. Discernment of the validity of these experiences, however, can be tricky.

I once had an intuitive dream of a doctor poking a huge needle into my college roommate's ring finger. When I awoke, I wondered if this was about me, since most dreams reflect the dreamer's unconscious. I had a strong sense it was not about me, so I called my friend who lived in another city. She expressed heartfelt gratitude that I called because she'd just undergone an anxiety producing procedure that involved a needle removing cancerous cells from her face. I wondered why my unconscious chose the ring finger rather than the cheek. Previously, we both had started new romantic relationships at the same time and enjoyed sharing how similarly they were unfolding. But mine resulted in an engagement and hers did not. I knew this upset her. My unconscious correctly picked up the distress of my friend's procedure but combined it with my memory of her being upset about not getting engaged. This showed me how psychological concerns may intrude and distort an authentic intuitive experience.

Whether these experiences are authentic or not, the best strategy is not to give them any importance, no matter how compelling they may be. Otherwise, you may get too attached to them and mistake them for the final goal. They can easily inflate your ego, leading you to say, "Wow, look how much I'm advancing!" You may seek out or push for similar experiences, as though feeding an addiction. You might get stuck in this place, unable to detach from their flashy and enticing nature of your experiences.

The Zen and Christian Orthodox teachers make surprisingly similar statements about ignoring these heightened experiences. Calling them *makyo* (fantasies, hallucinations), the Zen master Yasutani, says it well:

> Never be tempted into thinking that these phenomena are real or that the visions themselves have any meaning. To see a beautiful vision of a Bodhisattva does not mean that you are any nearer becoming one yourself, any more than a dream of being a millionaire means that you are any richer when you awake. Hence there is no reason to feel elated about such *makyo*. And similarly, whatever horrible monsters may appear to you, there is no cause whatever for alarm. Above all, do not allow yourself to be enticed by visions of the Buddha, or of gods blessing you, or communicating a divine message, or by *makyo* involving prophecies which turn out to be true. This is to squander your energies in the foolish pursuit of the inconsequential.[201]

The phrase "foolish pursuit of the inconsequential" beautifully summarizes the danger associated with these phenomena. You can easily veer off the true path if you take them too seriously.

A similar warning appears in the Christian Orthodox book, the *Philokalia* and quoted in *The Way of a Pilgrim*.

> During the time of contemplation, one is to avoid every kind of dreaming, and is not to imagine or receive any kind of vision of light, of a saint, an angel, or of Christ. The Fathers warn strongly about this because the power of imagination could easily personify the ideas of the mind and the inexperienced could be lured by these images, regard them as visions of grace, and so give in to self-deception.[202]

Adyashanti aptly calls visions or voices by-products and warns about getting too attached to them. Jack Kornfield, in *A Path with Heart,* calls them side effects.[203]

Several years ago, a young man visited me at our retreat center to discuss his interest in different states of consciousness, out-of-body experiences, and finding the meaning of the images he visualized. He believed them essential for his spiritual growth. I told him that his professed desire for marriage and children would serve him far better on the spiritual path than these other pursuits. Meeting the challenges of everyday life is more conducive to developing your spiritual life than dwelling on such fascinating, yet fleeting experiences.

Progress Indicators

Although spiritual teachers warn about the dangers of becoming attached to, or seeking out, these heightened experiences, they nevertheless affirm that such experiences usually reflect progress in your practice. Even though Yasutani warns about getting caught up in *makyo,* he claims, "Such visions are certainly a sign that you are at a crucial point in your sitting, and that if you exert yourself to the utmost, you can surely experience *kensho* [enlightenment]."[204] Jack Kornfield in *A Path with Heart* claims they "show a breakdown in the old and small structures of our being [which is progress] but they do not in themselves produce wisdom."[205] The Sufis would say that these experiences do have a reality but only exist on an intermediary plane of consciousness prior to the ultimate level of Union or Formlessness.

Don't be discouraged if you don't have any of these enticing experiences. Ultimately, they don't matter. They may come from a higher level of consciousness or not. They may indicate spiritual progress or not. The key is detachment, allowing them to pass without much further involvement. If they are authentic, they will positively change you without you thinking anymore about them. They may give you an understanding of the broader range of human experience. Without focusing on them, you may still catch a glimpse of the extent and grandeur of the spiritual journey.

Reflections on Illumination as
Heightened Awareness

1. What experiences have you had that showed an increase in your sensitivity to life? Do you feel your heart opening more? Has your intuition become sharper?

2. What is your view on the authenticity of the psychic powers mentioned in this chapter?

Chapter 11:
Light Extinguished–The Dark Night of the Soul

There can be no rebirth without a dark night of the soul, a total annihilation of all that you believed in and thought that you were.[206]

–Pir Vilayat Inayat Khan

The Dark Night of the Soul is one of the most difficult parts of the spiritual journey. After experiencing realms of brilliant light, a sense of a divine presence and radiant well-being, you might believe you've reached the pinnacle of your spiritual life. You might marvel at the increase in your creativity, intuition and understanding of the secrets of the universe, but all this expansion and bliss suddenly disappears during the dark night. Why? Because there are still more deep-seated attachments that were not entirely eliminated during the Purification Stage, and these prevent you from being completely free. You may have been able to take an active role in letting go of some attachments during Purification, but not so in the Dark Night. Any stripping away is passive. It's done *to* you.

What kinds of attachments are likely to remain that need to be stripped away? You might be too attached to your experiences of light, mistaking them for Ultimate Reality itself. You might have a secret pride or smug satisfaction in your spiritual accomplishments, thinking you are better and further along the journey than others. You might want to be the star pupil of your teacher. You might identify yourself secretly as the most spiritually advanced in your community and be upset if someone else takes that role. You might relish telling others about your spiritual experiences. You might find you want to control or fix what happens in your life rather than hand it over to the Great Mystery.[207]

All of these indicate your ego is still very much in play. Convinced you've reached a higher plateau than others, you still see yourself as separate from them. When you crave control of your life, particularly during hard times, rather than trusting in something higher than yourself, your will remains separate from the greater Will. You are not yet united with the All.

Perhaps you've wrestled with these thoughts and desires before and thought you had dealt with them. But the ego is tricky. It can hide for a while and then pop up again when you thought you sent it packing.

Some time ago, I recall merrily writing about the Dark Night and feeling satisfied with how the words flowed through me, when suddenly my computer quit, erasing all I had written. No pop-up window asked if I wanted to save my entries—the computer simply shut down. At first, I got angry, believing I would never recapture what I'd written. But then I had to laugh, because this occurrence was such a great metaphor for the Dark Night.

You may have encountered beautiful spiritual states of consciousness and felt a deep connection to the Divine as it flowed through your whole being. You may have endured and succeeded on your path to a certain point, feeling considerable satisfaction with your progress. Then suddenly all your previous spiritual experiences, sense of spiritual progress or ideas about the spiritual life are wiped away—an extremely disconcerting turn of events.

Characteristics

The Dark Night can affect all or most dimensions of your being. Visually, everything seems gray. Emotionally, you might feel bereft and abandoned. Energetically, your drive is lost. You may feel disconnected from your daily activities as if you were doing them robotically. Your meditations may seem flat. No longer are you able to access the peace and contentment that they usually bring. Spiritual books and retreats no longer appeal to you. Nothing excites. Any sense of Divine presence is absent. Mentally, you might question everything, wondering whether your previous experiences were real. You may doubt the validity and purpose of the spiritual life and wonder whether spiritual realization is simply a myth.

Psychologically, you might be confronted with issues that you didn't address during the Purification Stage. These might appear internally in the form of scary visions, dreams or taunting voices. Externally, these challenges may come in the form of difficult life challenges. Any lingering attachments are fair game.

The Dark Night takes an ax to your will. Sheer determination and effort will not make things change. Hard as you try, you can't reverse course or power your way through this stage. You can't manufacture the beautiful experiences you once had. No positive affirmations or glib spiritual rhetoric will make the darkness go away. There is no light. All hope is gone. You can only endure, surrender, be present to whatever arises and wait for grace to bring you out of the morass.

In *The End of Your World*, Adyashanti describes his experience: "I failed at meditating well; I failed at figuring out the truth. Everything I ever used to succeed spiritually failed. But at that moment of failure, that's when everything opens up."[208] This is not to say that you try to use defeat as a strategy for success. You can't give up and hope for the best. In this case, your ego orchestrates a surrender. This is different than when you come to a point in your spiritual development that you believe, with your whole being, that all your efforts have been in vain and all you can do is bow your head, stay quiet, and stop striving. One Buddhist text calls this "the rolling-up-the-mat" stage.[209]

This same sense of hopelessness and defeat also appears in the shamanic tradition, as illustrated in this passage from Carlos Castaneda's *The Eagle's Gift*.

He came to accept that an unconquerable pessimism over-
takes a warrior at a certain point on his path. A sense of defeat,

or perhaps more accurately, a sense of unworthiness, comes upon him almost unawares. . . . At such moments a lifelong training takes over, and the warrior enters into a state of unsurpassed humility; when the true poverty of his human resources becomes undeniable, the warrior has no recourse but to step back and lower his head.[210]

To add to the agony of defeat, a Dark Night experience can leave you feeling that the desolation and despair will never end. As St. Thérèse of Lisieux (1873–1897) wrote in *Story of the Soul*:

Then suddenly the fog about me seems to enter my very soul and fill it to such an extent that I cannot even find there the lovely picture I had formed of [heaven]; everything has disappeared!

When, weary of being enveloped by nothing but darkness, I try to comfort and encourage myself with the thought of the eternal life to come, it only makes matters worse. The very darkness seems to echo the voices of those who do not believe, and mocks at me: you dream of light and of a fragrant land; you dream of escaping one day from these mists in which you languish! Dream on, welcome death; it will not bring you what you hope; it will bring an even darker night, the night of nothingness![211]

St. Thérèse tried to have hope of future brightness and an end to her suffering, but such hopes were quickly squashed.

Depending on your personality, you may experience one dimension of the Dark Night more intensely than others. If you're a feeling type, your experience might be similar to losing a loved one with its accompanying grief and bewilderment. If you are more of a thinking type, the Dark Night might manifest as mental darkness and confusion. If you're the type that gets things done, you might feel paralyzed with no desire to do anything.

As true for other states in the spiritual journey, you might experience the Dark Night stage more than once. As oscillations occur between Purification and Illumination, so do they appear between Illumination and the Dark Night. They help dissolve your ego gradually. Sometimes you may briefly dip into the Dark Night—a mini dark night, if you will. You may go through a phase of despair and dissolution but emerge somewhat quickly to resume a connection with your spiritual life.

This happened to me when visiting the Mother Center of Yogananda's Self-Realization Fellowship in Los Angeles. Sitting on a bench in the outdoor circle where Yogananda used to teach, I suddenly felt my whole life was like straw. It had no substance and could be burned away without much fanfare. Overcome with agony, I couldn't stay seated any longer and quickly left the grounds. The feeling only lasted for a day, but it transformed me. I couldn't take my life as seriously as I had before.

Often, during the Dark Night, you feel you're going to die. This makes sense because the ego part of you *is* dying. Several times, I have felt like I was about to die. I wasn't suicidal or depressed; I just believed without much emotion that my life was about to end. Having been through this experience a few times, I now recognize my life is not ending, but only some part of me is ending. This awareness, however, doesn't diminish the emptiness and bewilderment I feel at the time.

Comparison of the Dark Night to the Dark Wood Stage and to Depression

What is the difference between the Dark Night and the Dark Wood? Both make you feel like nothing is happening, nothing inspires and you don't know your next step. You basically feel okay, however, when experiencing the Dark Wood—but not so in the Dark Night. In this state, everything, including the meaning of your existence, is questioned. The Dark Night comes upon those seekers who have had some initial awakening experience. The agony and grief are thereby heightened because the contrast between their earlier spiritual encounters and their present feelings of despair makes it so much harder to bear.

Some of the descriptions cited by individuals who go through the Dark Night may make you wonder if there's any difference between the

Dark Night and depression. Sometimes a person suffering from depression likens their experience to that of the Dark Night—they may feel the grayness, loss of energy, despair and deep questioning of life. Both can arise in spiritually developed persons. Although you might be able to discern whether it is one or the other based on your level of spiritual growth or your prior experience of the Illumination Stage, the distinction is not an easy one. I find it difficult to tease out the similarities and differences between the two. As soon as I think of one characteristic that is different about the Dark Night, I can find shades of it in those experiencing depression. More work needs to be done to discern the difference or relationship between the two.

External Challenges

One of the greatest external challenges you might experience during the Dark Night is a threat to your reputation. At this stage of your development, others might have noticed a peace about you, admired your wisdom or good deeds in the world. You might be known as an inspiring spiritual person. What would it be like, then, if you suddenly became persona non grata, and those who had admired you now held you in contempt? How would you respond? Would your ego be sufficiently aligned with your essential self that you wouldn't be bothered by this challenge?

John of the Cross became a persona non grata when his fellow, non-reformed Carmelite monks put him in prison because they felt his work for the reform movement disrupted the whole order. For nine months, he was confined to a six-by-ten-foot room with a small two-inch peephole for a window. He could only read at midday by standing on a bench. He was not allowed to change clothes and so was covered with lice. In the summer, sores from beatings by his imprisoners became worm-infested. He was given only water, pieces of bread and sardines to eat, developing dysentery as a result. He also suffered psychologically, doubting the rightness of the reform and his defiance of the General of his Order. He worried that if he had been wrong, he would be separated from God forever. No wonder he was the first to coin the term "dark night of the soul." Despite all this, he composed beautiful poetry that would become the basis of three of his major mystical works. He became a saint and light to the world.[212]

This example of John of the Cross is an extreme one. I recoil every time I read this. Thankfully, most seekers entering the Dark Night don't endure such severe suffering. Before getting too discouraged or overwhelmed by the many dire characteristics of the Dark Night, it may be helpful to inject a little humor.

While she traveled to one of her monasteries in the pouring rain, Teresa of Ávila's cart got stuck in the mud while crossing a river, causing her to perilously continue on foot. She thrust her fist in the air and yelled to God, "If this is how you treat your friends, no wonder you have so few of them!"[213] I am sure those who experience the Dark Night feel the same way, although they may not even be sure there is a God to be angry with.

Purpose

What is the purpose of the despair and suffering experienced during the Dark Night? Put simply, it's to free you from yourself. Your self-consciousness gets stripped away so you can now only think and act from the viewpoint of oneness—from the greater energies operating in the Universe. Despite his ordeal, John of the Cross says:

> Therefore, O spiritual soul, when you see your desires obscured, your emotions arid and constrained, and your faculties bereft . . . be not afflicted by this, but rather consider it a great happiness since God is freeing you from yourself and taking the matter from your hands.[214]

You'll no doubt find it difficult to feel happy when undergoing the challenges of the Dark Night, but if you can keep his words in your mind, you might find it more bearable.

Freeing you from your ego self includes eliminating any of your arrogance, self-importance or belief that you know what constitutes the spiritual life. The Oxherding pictures do not include a separate entry for the Dark Night of the soul, but the opening lines of the eighth Zen Oxherding picture[215] clearly show its effects:

All delusive feelings have perished, and ideas of holiness too have vanished. He lingers not in [the state of "I am a] Buddha," and he passes quickly on through [the stage of "And now I have purged myself of the proud feeling [I am] not Buddha."[216]

Knowing this passage was written many centuries ago, I'm amazed how little human nature has changed. Perhaps you have noticed, as I have, that after experiencing an expanded state of consciousness your ego quickly comes in and takes credit for it. The Zen practitioner moves beyond this situation. His ego, with its self-importance, has now been laid to rest.

Outcome

What are the results of going through the trials of the Dark Night of the Soul? One of the best descriptions of the Dark Night's aftermath appears in Sirkar van Stolk's *Memories of a Sufi Sage: Hazrat Inayat Khan.* Van Stolk observed his master, HIK, at close range over a number of years. At one point, HIK went into a deep period of meditation during which he experienced all human suffering, not only of those living on earth, but also, according to the account, of those suffering in states of consciousness after death. Van Stolk described the aftermath of such a Dark Night experience:

When he emerged from this great trial, none of his shortcomings were left in him. To those of us who had known him before, the change was most marked. There was something superhuman now in his majesty and grandeur. Although his feet trod the same earth, there was a quality about him which I can only describe as cosmic. Every particle of his being was now given up to service as a superb channel for the Divine.[217]

Take heart! There's a sublime outcome to the Dark Night. Having passed through its trials, these seekers are gloriously and profoundly changed. Their thoughts and actions are no longer personal but now align with the Divine flow. They have moved into the Unitive stage—the subject of the next chapter.

Reflections on the Dark Night of the Soul

1. Does knowledge of the Dark Night of the Soul scare or discourage you?

2. What challenges have you experienced that threaten your ego?

3. After reading this chapter, do you view failure differently?

4. What spiritual attachments do you still have?

5. Does the purpose of the Dark Night make sense to you?

Chapter 12:
Everlasting Light and Beyond–
Unitive Stage

The ineffable sweetness of perfect union cannot
be described with the tongue, which is a finite thing.

Lovely beyond loveliness is the home of the soul in perfect
union with Me.

Nothing stands between us because she has become one
thing with Me.

–God speaking to Catherine of Siena[218]

The Unitive Stage marks the beginning of a totally new state of consciousness. Here you attain the perfect union with the Radiant All that you have sought consciously or unconsciously throughout your spiritual life. Different spiritual traditions point to this stage with their own terminology—final enlightenment, finding your True Nature, self-realization, spiritual marriage between lover and Beloved, end of the cycles of rebirth, or abiding awakening. While these terms are not precisely equivalent, they all circle around the same idea of oneness. The deepest dimension of the Unitive stage lies beyond all words and concepts. Here, the varying spiritual traditions use similar language such as emptiness, no-thingness, void or darkness to describe this reality.

The End of Your Seeking

During the Illuminative Stage, you may have experienced some of the same elements such as universal knowledge, bliss, peace and light that also appear in the Unitive Stage. But now these qualities are heightened, more permanent and everlasting. Gone are the oscillations between the other stages. The separation between the seeker and the Radiant All, which exists in the Illuminative Stage, also disappears. Seekers no longer think, speak and act from their own consciousness but from a wider, all-encompassing one. Although Illumination brings intermittent experiences of oneness, the Unitive Stage ushers in a major shift in consciousness, in which you abide constantly in this state. Any challenges that you face are mitigated by your continual awareness of—and connection to—the Divine or Universal Love.

John of the Cross in his *Spiritual Canticle* indicates other results of the unitive stage:

- All digressions of the mind have ended.

- Anger and desire for pleasure have been brought under control.

- Memory, will and understanding have reached a state of perfection because they now align with the Divine mind.

- All troublesome and disruptive acts of the four emotions of joy, hope, grief and fear have been eliminated.[219]

That is something to work toward. I'd love to be free of disruptive thoughts and emotions. Note: John of the Cross doesn't say your thoughts and emotions disappear, only their disruptive power. After all, you're still human. There's always room for more growth.

Keep in mind that the union of the soul with the Radiant All already exists at the deepest level of your being. The apex of the spiritual journey is to become fully conscious of this union and then act from this place of oneness. The Unitive Stage most often appears after many years of spiritual growth, with all its glories and challenges. Bit by bit, the ego dissolves until the seeker's will becomes completely aligned with the Divine Will or Flow of the Universe. Few reach this spiritual peak, but it's the pole star for all who are interested in the spiritual life.

Sublime descriptions of this stage help you stay on track, and your own glimpses during moments of awe or deep contemplation kindle your desire for dwelling in this state permanently. Although your purifications, detachments and spiritual practices help you approach this stage, the arrival is ultimately a grace.

Even though the experience of this stage is beyond words, spiritual masters from various traditions give compelling descriptions of the unitive state. What they tell us is truly inspiring. I find it useful to view this stage through the diverse lenses of Contemporary Spirituality, Zen Buddhism, Christianity and Sufism. The subtle differences in the perspectives of these traditions provide a fuller and clearer sense of this elevated level of consciousness.

Contemporary Lens: Adyashanti and Gangaji

In *The End of Your World*, Adyashanti describes the Unitive Stage, which he calls full awakening, as seeing from the perspective of oneness all the time. "From this awakened perspective, there isn't any separation anywhere—not in the world, not in the universe, not in all the universes everywhere."[220]

He continues by saying true awakening ushers in the end of your seeking, the end of your identity as a seeker and the end of your idea of spirituality or the spiritual path. These concepts may have been useful at one time as a means of reaching the goal but are now obsolete. As the Buddhists teach, it's good to have a boat to take you to the other shore, but once you're there, you'd be silly to carry it around with you.

According to Adyashanti, even though your ego has surrendered to a higher Power, your personality remains. You simply no longer identify with it. Rather, it is an instrument through which the Radiant Oneness flows. "Life has a part to play through me, and so I play the part. I'm in union with the part life plays through me. The part changes all the time, moment to moment, but that's what I'm in union with. I'm no longer arguing with life."[221]

The contemporary spiritual teacher, Gangaji, share her understanding of the enlightened state. Some claim she is not fully enlightened, but what she says about this state rings true. She agrees with

Adyashanti that a person reaching this stage is free of all identities. When asked if she is a guru, she responded, "No." To the surprise of her questioner, she continued by saying, "I'm not a human being . . . I'm not a woman, and yet I have experiences of being a human and experiences of being a woman. But who I am is so much deeper."[222] Like Adyashanti, she acknowledges that even though she lives from this unitary state of consciousness, she still has a personality. She still has distinctive characteristics and qualities such as a loving heart and sense of humor. She also still has her flaws. She just doesn't identify with her personality but with the Divine within her. I love observing various spiritual teachers either in person or through the media to see how they express this highest state in their own unique way. No two are alike, but the energy emanating from them has a similar effect—to transform those lucky enough to be in their presence.

Both Adyashanti and Gangaji admit that even though your ego is no longer running the show, the latent tendencies or fixations inherent in your psyche can surface even when you're fully awakened. What does this look like?

When these latent tendencies arise, there's no fuel to feed the impulse. There's no story around what's arising, so they die right then, having no place to go. They can be stimulated in a variety of ways, such as seeing a movie, feeling a bodily pain, facing tension in a relationship, or whatever situation activates your past wounds and programming. These fixations are not the problem. They will arise in anyone, enlightened or not.

The problem is believing these latent tendencies are a problem. In his blog, de Mellow talked about how he was depressed before becoming enlightened and is still depressed afterward. He's just not attached to the idea of being depressed.[223] This implies that those experiencing union or abiding awakening simply accept "what is" without judging any experience as good or bad. This requires tremendous faith that "all will be well and every kind of thing will be well," as Julian of Norwich proclaims.[224] For me, the spiritual journey entails a movement from a distrust to a total trust of "what is."

Spiritual realization or the Unitive Stage has been mischaracterized as a mystical or trance state. On the contrary, Adyashanti finds that most people live in a trance every day because they don't see what's truly real. Rather, he says, enlightenment is an "unaltered state of consciousness."[225] He affirms the Buddhist idea that spiritual realization is a deep naturalness and simplicity, a "dying into the ordinary which is extraordinary!"[226] It's experiencing every ordinary moment as miraculous. As the Zen master Layman Pang-yun (740–808) states:

What I do every day
Is nothing special:
I simply stumble around.
What I do is not thought out,
Where I go is unplanned.
No matter who tries to leave their mark,
The hills and dales are not impressed.
Collecting firewood and carrying water
Are prayers that reach the gods.[227]

Gangaji also points to the ordinariness of the enlightened state.

My daily life looks like any other life. It probably looks more boring than a lot of lives. I love to spend time with my husband. I like to go for walks and read books and go to the movies. I read two newspapers a day. Doing laundry is the only housework I enjoy, and ironing is one of my favorite things because I find it relaxing. I spend time shopping—not that I love to shop, but I do like good food and nice clothes and nice things. So you can see I don't live a saintly life. Everyone who knows me well knows I am not a saint. But this ordinary life is filled with love. It is filled with peace.[228]

I appreciate this description of how individuals who are in touch with the ocean of love all the time can still live in the world in ordinary ways. They are both ordinary and extraordinary. Gangaji exclaims, "In the ordinariness of you and me, there's a sublime presence of Truth."[229]

Zen Buddhist Lens

Having been trained in the Zen tradition, Adyashanti frames much of his description of enlightenment in similar ways to the Oxherding pictures.

Eighth Oxherding Picture:
Both Ox and Self Forgotton

The eighth picture denotes an empty circle. The Ox, which symbolizes enlightenment or your True Nature, and the seeker are now one. Distinctions, words or images no longer exist—just empty space, which designates the Radiant All or the Ground of all things.

> Whip, rope, Ox and man alike belong to Emptiness.
> So vast and infinite the azure sky
> that no concept of any sort can reach it.
> Over a blazing fire a snowflake cannot survive.[230]

I love the imagery of the last line. In the Unitive Stage, words, concepts or images beautifully and gently disappear.

Ninth Oxherding Picture:
Return to the Source

The eighth picture of the empty circle depicts the Absolute or Real, which is beyond all forms (Divine Transcendence); the ninth points to the Absolute within form (Divine Immanence). Rather than an empty circle, the ninth Oxherding picture, titled *Return to the Source*, portrays a scene from nature, conveying that the One is present in the many. The blue waters and green mountains are perfect as they are.

> From the very beginning there has not been so much as a speck of dust [to mar the intrinsic Purity]. He observes the waxing and waning of life in the world while abiding unassertively in a state of unshakable serenity. This [waxing and waning]

is no phantom or illusion [but a manifestation of the Source].
Why then is there need to strive for anything? The waters are
blue, the mountains are green. Alone with himself, he observes
things endlessly changing.[231]

At this stage, the enlightened seeker dwells in the Divine Purity
that underlies and is part of all things. This Purity, which also resides
in you, cannot be defiled no matter how much you have suffered, been
abused or betrayed. Touching such Purity eliminates any need to fix or
change things. Everything can be accepted just as it is. The person in
this stage sees the beauty of the blue sky and tall, graceful trees rooted
in white snow. She also experiences the love and vitality permeating all
life, including the homeless, the sick and all those who are suffering.

If you're having difficulties accepting any unpleasant challenges that arise, Pema Chödrön advocates leaning into what you want to
avoid, being fully present to it in your body and emotions and then becoming aware of others who experience similar challenges. This method shifts the originating experience for the better and induces greater
compassion.[232]

The reference to "waxing and waning" in the commentary on the
ninth picture reminds us that the nature of immanent Reality is movement. Not disturbed by the endless change, the enlightened one harmo-
nizes—and is united with—the flow.

Richard Baker, a student of Shunryū Suzuki, touches these same
points when he describes the experience of his enlightened teacher as
one who actualizes perfect freedom. The flow of his consciousness is
not from "the fixed repetitive patterns of usual self-centered consciousness, but rather arises spontaneously and naturally from the actual circumstances of the present." Such freedom induces a joyfulness, buoy-
ancy, insight, compassion and serenity.[233]

Christian Lens: Deification and Spiritual Marriage

The Christian mystics express the union of the soul with the Divine in
two basic ways—impersonal and transcendent (deification); or personal and intimate (spiritual marriage). Both describe the surrender of self

and the emergence of freedom. Meister Eckhart belongs to the "union as deification" camp. He writes: "When the soul has lost her nature in the Oneness, we can no longer speak of a 'soul,' but of immeasurable Being."[234]

John of the Cross expresses this union in the intimate terms of spiritual marriage in his famous poem, "On a Dark Night." It outlines the complete trajectory of the spiritual journey, but I cite only the stanzas relevant to understanding the description of Unitive stage in terms of lover and Beloved.

> Oh, night that joined Beloved with lover,
> Lover transformed in the Beloved! . . .
> I remained, lost in oblivion;
> My face I reclined on the Beloved.
> All ceased and I abandoned myself,
> Leaving my cares forgotten among the lilies.[235]

The phrase "I abandoned myself," indicates that the seeker has now surrendered his individual consciousness to the All, and yet the soul somehow remains in a "transformed" state.

Just as the other traditions explain how the mystic's thoughts and actions stem from this state of oneness, so also does the Christian mystical tradition. In his *Living Flame of Love*, St. John of the Cross elaborates on the mechanics of this union with the Beloved.

> So the understanding of the soul is now the understanding of God; and its will is the will of God; and its memory is the memory of God; and its delight is the delight of God; and the substance of the soul, although it is not the Substance of God, for it cannot be changed, is nevertheless united in Him and absorbed in Him. . . . And thus the death of this soul is changed into the life of God.[236]

Christian mystics differ in the way they address the metaphysical question of what happens to the soul during the Unitive Stage. Some writers suggest the mystic's soul or True Nature becomes so absorbed in the Radiant All that it ceases to exist. Others suggest some essential quality of the soul remains but is transformed.[237]

The first possibility is symbolized by a drop of water in the ocean, the second by an iron in the fire.[238] As iron is placed in fire, it changes from cool to hot, and from blackness to radiant light. Yet, it still maintains its properties of iron-ness. This second view implies that the mystical stage of union involves transformation but not erasure of one's very nature. Most Christian mystics favor this view.

Sometimes both seemingly opposite viewpoints of what happens to the soul in the Unitive Stage—disappearing into oneness or retaining some essential quality—appear in the same paragraph. Louis de Blois (1506–1566) writes:

> It is a great thing, an exceeding great thing, in the times of this exile to be joined to God in the divine light by a mystical and denuded union, [The soul] melts away into God [Type 1]. It is united to God without any medium and becomes one spirit with Him, is transformed and changed into Him, as iron placed in the fire is changed into fire, without ceasing to be iron [Type 2].[239]

Realizing how contradictory his own words appear, de Blois embraces this mystery by resorting to paradoxical language. The soul "loses itself in the infinite solitude and darkness of the Godhead; but so to lose itself is rather to find itself."[240] I interpret these seemingly contradictory statements to mean that unitive consciousness is so vast and all-encompassing that it holds all the opposites, all the concepts that our human minds can and cannot comprehend, and all that lies beyond anything that can be expressed in words.

You might think the Unitive Stage is static because the dance among the stages no longer occurs. Yet, as Adyashanti and the Zen Oxherding pictures have shown, the Radiant All is dynamic and continually emerging. The Christian mystics agree. John of the Cross in his *Spiritual Canticle* claims that despite all the experiences of all the mystics throughout the ages, there is always more learning and growth because the Divine is infinite. "For He is like an abundant mine with many recesses containing treasures, of which, for all [who] try to fathom them, the end and the bottom is never reached; rather in each recess, [seekers] continue to find new veins of new riches on all sides."[241]

I love this metaphor. Imagine going into a mine and finding rubies to your right, emeralds to your left, and diamonds farther along your way. Even better, your discoveries continue without end. This viewpoint of growth within the Unitive state, accounts for the different degrees of spiritual attainment in different spiritual teachers. There's always more! Perhaps the struggles and challenges of the spiritual life are worth it.

The Sufi Lens

Like these other traditions, Sufism recognizes the same elements of the Unitive Stage, such as seeing the oneness in all things and becoming united with the Divine. As a spirituality of the heart, it views the Radiant All not as a distant overseer of the universe, but as the personal Beloved. In the Unitive Stage the lover and Beloved become united in one, as HIK so beautifully describes:

> I consider it good fortune when
> Thou art alone with me,
> but when I am not there at all,
> I think it the greatest blessing.[242]

Descriptions of the Unitive Stage find their captivating expression in Sufi poetry and stories. In his poem, "Laughing at the Word Two," Hafiz conveys this union in a delightful way.

> Only
> That Illumined
> One
>
> Who keeps
> Seducing the formless into form
>
> Had the charm to win my
> Heart.
>
> Only a Perfect One
>
> Who is always
> Laughing at the word

Two
Can make you know
Of
Love.[243]

A man knocked on a door. "Who is there?" asked God.
"Me," replied the man. "Go away then," said God.
The man left and wandered in the arid desert until he
realized his error and returned to the door.
He knocked again, "Who's there?" asked God.
"You," answered the man. "Then come in,"
replied God. "There's no room here for two."[244]

–Freke, *The Wisdom of Sufi Stages*

In addition to poems and stories, the main Sufi practice of *dhikr* (Arabic) or *zikr* (Persian), can elicit a state of oneness. *Zikr* means remembrance—a going back to the Source. Using bodily motions, the practitioner continually repeats the words "La ilaha illa 'llah hu," which is usually translated as "there is no god but God" or "there is no reality but Divine Reality." "La" means "no." In the practice, you at first might be saying "no" to what is false; "no" to all that does not serve your True Nature; "no" to pettiness; "no" to stuckness; "no" to words and concepts; "no" to all that is not Allah. After repeating this phrase many times, you may begin to see the real meaning of the zikr—that all reality is Allah.[245] As the Qur'an states: "Wherever you turn, there is the face of Allah." (2:115)[246] Allah is beyond and within all things, both transcendent and immanent.

The Sufi practice of *fana*, which means annihilation of the separate self, consists of a three-step process that leads to ever-widening spheres of consciousness. First, the student surrenders into—or unites with—the consciousness of her teacher (*fana-fi-Shaykh*), then to the consciousness of the Rasul or worldwide teacher (*fana-fi-Rasul*), such as Mohammed, Jesus or Buddha. Finally, the seeker totally abandons the illusory self and unites with Allah (*fana-fi-Allah*).[247]

The renowned philosopher, mystic and poet Ibn 'Arabi (1165–

1240) expresses the mechanics of the union between lover and Beloved in terms very similar to John of the Cross as quoted above. "When you realize the mystery of Oneness with the Divine . . . you will understand that all your actions are His actions, and your essence is His essence, and all your attributes belong to Him."[248]

How does the enlightened Sufi appear to others? In *Memories of a Sufi Sage,* Sirkar van Stolk shares his impression of HIK after he reached the Unitive Stage, as one having a magnificent presence who is now free from all the limitations of his personality. "To say he is kind, or unselfish or modest, simply does not touch the truth. It is like trying to encompass the power and beauty of an ocean with the term "pretty."[249]

Human and Divine

When you live from unitary consciousness and all your thoughts and actions are divine ones you might expect that all your problems and challenges will disappear. This is not the case. Those who attain this stage are subjected to the vicissitudes of human life like everyone else. They withstand illnesses, loss of loved ones, and other challenges. Not only do they experience their own trials, but they are also more sensitive to the suffering of others.

Adyashanti has been through several rounds of a painful and unknown (at least to the public) illness and Gangaji had to deal with her husband's brief infidelity. Lama Tsultrim Allione felt crushed after the sudden death of her beloved husband; she went into retreat for months to integrate and heal her wounded heart. In *Just Like You,* Gangaji relates how her heart breaks every time when she reads the newspaper, witnesses someone missing a chance to be awakened or sees the preciousness of her grandchildren.[250]

What aids the enlightened ones through these difficulties is their direct experience of the love that underlies all existence. They know that these happenings are part of something greater, a higher consciousness. In many cases they are able to move through these upsets faster. Adyashanti finds he can work through these challenges almost instantaneously. That doesn't mean they go away; they just don't have much of an effect. As Gangaji claims:

Moments of discomfort and unhappiness come, but those moments are always on an ocean of peace. The moment pass, but
the ocean of love and peace doesn't go anywhere. I know it to
be bottomless. Endless. Limitless. I know it to be who I am.[251]

Beyond Light/The Divine Dark

The deepest dimension of the Unitive Stage is beyond all words and
concepts. Here, the varying spiritual traditions uncannily use similar
language to describe this Reality. References to concepts such as formless, wordless, nothingness, emptiness, void and darkness appear in
writings from both East and West. As Meister Eckhart says, "A master
says whoever speaks of God in any likeness, speaks impurely of him.
But to speak of God with nothing is to speak of him correctly."[252] These
terms help us to see that the final destination is beyond anything we can
possibly fathom. At the same time, such descriptions may erroneously
convey a sense of no reality or substance.

In contemplating these mystical writings, you might wonder if
the end of the journey or final enlightenment is really nothingness. You
might think that going beyond all forms and concepts would mean nothing is happening, perhaps resulting in boredom. It is not nothingness
but no-thingness. Dionysius the Aeropagite (late fifth to early sixth century) calls it the "superessential Radiance of the Divine Darkness."[253]
Adyashanti calls it radiant emptiness[254] and the Sufis sometimes refer
to it as the midnight sun or black light.[255] All these expressions are paradoxical, and they need to be. No one concept can accurately describe
this Reality. However, such language does convey an aliveness and
fullness that is far from boring.

Moving from the known into a deep place of unknowing can
seem endless. Keep going and you'll reach the goal, as verse 35 of
the Buddhist Heart Sutra proclaims: "Gone, gone, gone beyond, gone
completely beyond, Enlightenment, so be it!"[256] The empty circle of
the eighth Oxherding picture conveys in a simple way this sense of
no-thingness as does Chapter 14 of the *Tao Te Ching*:

Look, it cannot be seen—it is beyond form.
Listen, it cannot be heard—it is beyond sound.
Grasp, it cannot be held—it is intangible.
These three are indefinable;
Therefore, they are joined in one.[257]

Byron, a source for my dissertation, made a similar statement.

It is difficult to describe this realm of silence. I experienced
no images. I am there in silence, but I am not differentiated
from the silence. In some sense there is no I. There is a deep
profound peace and a sense of primordial reality. I called it
The Real; I could call it being or non-being, but I couldn't call
it unreal.[258]

For me, "a profound peace and sense of primordial reality" reveals a sense of all-encompassing expansiveness—the infinite sky—
that is far from boring or nothingness.

John van Ruysbroeck, a Christian monk, describes "the abysmal
waylessness of God" as "so dark and so unconditioned that it swallows
up within itself every divine way and activity." This makes me think of
a black hole that absorbs everything in its overpowering gravitational
force. We may view black holes as mathematical certainties, but mystics experience the darkness as something sublime, as divinity itself.
Ruysbroeck continues by saying, "This is the dark silence in which all
lovers lose themselves."[259]

As described in *Proof of Heaven,* the neurosurgeon Eben Alexander (b.1953) encountered the divine dark toward the end of a week-
long coma. Even though the part of his brain that controls thought and
emotion had been attacked by a rare illness, he experienced cognitive
awareness and transcending experiences.

I continued moving forward and found myself entering an immense void, completely dark, infinite in size, yet also infinitely
comforting. Pitch black as it was, it was also brimming over
with light: a light that seemed to come from a brilliant orb that
I now sensed near me. . . . Later, when I was back here in the

world, I found a quotation by the seventeenth century Christian poet, Henry Vaughn that came close to describing this place—this vast, inky-black core that was the home of the Divine itself. "There is, some say, in God a deep but dazzling darkness..." That was it, exactly: an inky darkness that was also full to brimming with light.[260]

You would think encountering this vast, immense void would be scary or overwhelming, but Alexander found it comforting. Such descriptions are the closest that words can come to conveying the nature of Absolute Reality.

The Mountain Top

Even though these different traditions have different flavors, they all seem to point to the same core experience of oneness. Generally, those trained in the Eastern traditions describe this stage in more impersonal ways—awakening, life, consciousness, freedom, truth, naturalness and purity. Most often, Christianity and Sufism use more personal and intimate terms—love, lover, Beloved, soul, union and God.

All these traditions claim the person in this stage no longer thinks and acts from their own individual self-awareness but from a unitive, overarching state of consciousness. All experience a deeper reality of peace, fullness, endlessness and limitlessness that goes beyond their personality. All flow with this greater Reality, experiencing but no longer impeded by life's challenges. They live both ordinary and extraordinary lives. As seekers move more deeply into the Unitive Stage, they encounter a Reality described as dark, empty, full and beyond words. At this point the wording between the traditions appears strikingly similar.

The Unitive Stage or Enlightenment has two dimensions—the seekers' mystical union with the Radiant All, and their concurrent effect as powerhouses in the world. This chapter has focused on the first dimension. The following chapter examines the effect of the enlightened individual in the world.

Reflections on the Unitive Stage

1. Contemplate the statement attributed to Anthony de Mello, "enlightenment is absolute cooperation with the inevitable."

2. Where does anxiety about your imperfection arise in your life?

3. At what times have you experienced the "extraordinary in the ordinary"?

4. Can you touch that place of purity in you that can never be defiled?

5. Exercise: Inhale—imagine a floorless and shoreless ocean. Exhale—imagine you are a drop dissolving into the vast ocean. Notice how you feel. Perhaps more relaxed, a sense of unwinding and connecting with all.

Chapter 13:
Becoming a Light in the World

The true mystic is not a devotee lost in
ecstatic communion with the One,
or a reclusive saint who avoids others. The true mystic
lives alongside other people—coming and going,
eating and sleeping, buying and selling, marrying and chatting
—but not for a moment does he forget God.

–Abu sa'id ibn Abi-L-Khayr (967–1049)[261]

No matter where you are in your spiritual development, you can have a positive effect on the world. The last part of this chapter explains how you can beneficially affect your environment, even if you're just a beginner on the path. But first, let's examine the superstars—those living in the Illuminative or Unitive Stages of consciousness—to discover their impact on the world.

Surprisingly, these mystics can uplift the world whether they are fully engaged in everyday life or secluded in monasteries or caves, and whether they're known or unknown. In the opening quotation, Abi-L-Kahyr expresses the Sufi view that the mystic's spiritual growth and subsequent impact on the world is best when living in the world. Other spiritual traditions find that living apart from the world is more beneficial to their spiritual growth. Either way, individuals at these higher stages of consciousness leave a profound mark on the world.

What causes these mystics to be so effective in the world?

- They're in touch with the energetic source of Reality and radiate energy to all.

- Like a laser, they are totally focused on the present moment without any care for the results of their actions.

- Their actions are in accord with actions of the Radiant All.

- They require less sleep and so have more time for both contemplation and action.

- Their compassion for all sentient beings moves them to help those in need.

Effect of Monastics, Hermits and Meditators on the World

It's easier to understand how mystics living in the world can perform significant works beneficial to humankind and the planet. What about those living in monasteries or caves, like the rishis in the Himalayas? If they live isolated from the world, from centers of population or the daily struggles of the human journey, how can they make a positive difference in the world? This can occur in several ways.

First, those who live in a monastery or convent are still part of a community of monks whose members learn from those among them who have attained greater states of awareness. When they become heads of their orders, they serve as both administrative leaders and spiritual guides to the other monks or nuns. Sometimes they become spokespersons for their tradition in the public domain. Thich Nhat Hanh, Brother David Steindl-Rast, Pema Chödrön, and Sr. Joan Chittister are well-known examples today. They have each spent most or all their life in a monastery, but now have a tremendous effect on the world through their teachings and writings.

A second way sequestered seekers can be of use to the world is through their developed sense of intuition. I knew a nun who worked with the police to locate missing persons. Her heightened intuitive ability enabled her to know where a person could be found. No one seeing her in religious garb, praying the hours and living the monastic life would suspect she had served in such a public role.

Third, individuals who spend time in meditation and prayer can transform the world. Some rigorous studies of Transcendental Meditation™ prove this point. When a certain number of advanced TM meditators are sent to a city, the crime rate initially goes down only to rise again once they've left.[262] For example, violent crime decreased by 23 percent in Washington, D.C, over a two-month period during the time TM meditators lived there and then subsequently increased after they left. The amazed chief of police said the only way a 20 percent decline in crime rate would ordinarily occur would be if there were twenty inches of snow on the ground.[263] If the pool of TM meditators is large enough, the uplifting vibration they create resonates with and transforms others, similar to how a tuning fork works.

Those living in monasteries or caves often practice remote or intercessory prayer. Studies show that this type of prayer is remarkably effective. In his book, *Healing Words,* Larry Dossey, M.D.[264] lists 131 experiments in which researchers remotely tried to positively affect living organisms ranging from humans to mice, fungi and yeast. They found seventy-seven of the trials had statistically significant results.[265] In light of this evidence, Dossey concluded that he needed to pray for his patients.

Please note: In viewing reality as an energy field, rather than a field in which sentient beings are separated by space, I don't see prayer as necessarily imploring some remote deity to produce a desired outcome. Rather, I view prayer, given the right concentration, as the creation of a specific ripple in the energy field, which can in turn positively affect a particular outcome.

These studies on meditation and prayer illustrate how individuals living in seclusion or monastic communities practicing meditation or prayer can benefit the world. Perhaps this knowledge is an incentive for you to start or continue your meditation or prayer practice. It can change both you and the world around you.

Effect of Mystics Living in the World

Without doubt, mystics living in the world—in the Illuminative or Unitive Stages—have had an enormous influence. In some cases, their impact stems from actual works they have done in the physical realm. In almost all cases, their very presence made a lasting impression on those they encountered. The consciousness of these beings extends beyond history, beyond their life on earth.

A clear historical example of great works stemming from awakened consciousness in Christianity is the experience of the apostles at Pentecost (Acts 2:1-13).[266] Prior to this event and after the death of Jesus, the apostles felt afraid, fearing they too would be similarly persecuted. Huddled together for the Jewish feast of Shavuot, they experienced a great influx of energy (the Holy Spirit) descend upon them with tongues of fire emerging from their heads. I interpret this event as a full kundalini awakening for each of the apostles. Suddenly, they were no longer afraid and found they could speak in many languages, perform wonders and miracles, and preach "the good news" far and wide. From this small group of individuals, emboldened by the power and illumination of the Spirit, came a worldwide movement known as Christianity.

Having researched and written an article on women Christian mystics,[267] I am most familiar with their lives and work. In Chapter 9, I introduced the creativity and prophetic ability of Hildegaard of Bingen. Two more examples—Bridget of Sweden (1303–1373), and Teresa of Ávila provide a window into the powerful work of mystics in the world.

Bridget of Sweden was a visionary, a prophet and a spiritual guide, as well as a mother of eight. She denounced the corruption in the Church and chastised the Swedish king and his court for their lack of concern for the subjects they ruled. She predicted the black plague for her country if their policies didn't change. Later in life, she wrote her own monastic rule and established a religious order consisting of men and women who lived separately but prayed together.[268]

Teresa of Ávila also addressed the corruption in the Church and became the motivating force for reform of her Carmelite order. Responding to the increasingly social nature of convents, Teresa sought to return to frequent meditation and prayer, vegetarian meals, living in simple quarters and daily meetings with the head mistress. Implementing these guidelines of discipline and simplicity, she founded her own convent plus twenty-three others along with two monasteries. This meant negotiating property deals, contracts and licenses; supervising the building or repair of proposed living quarters; and winning over the local authorities to her cause—all very worldly activities. Her spiritual writings show her astute understanding of psychological processes accompanying spiritual development, particularly her most famous work, *Interior Castle*.[269]

Hazrat Inayat Khan is a modern example of a spiritual master who has had a major impact on the world. He brought Sufism to the West in 1910, founded an international Sufi order now called the *Inayatiyya, a Sufi Path of Spiritual Liberty*, and lectured widely in both Europe and America. These lectures were compiled into numerous books that are still available.

Many spiritual teachers living today also have a profound impact. These include Adyashanti, Jack Kornfield, Rupert Spira, Eckhart Tolle, Tara Brach, Mirabai Starr and Starhawk. They write books, offer retreats, and give numerous talks and broadcasts. I'm amazed how frequently they can produce such inspired teachings over so many years. Surely, an outpouring of higher energies flows through them to the benefit of many.

Not only do spiritual masters execute works that can be seen, but they also work on levels that cannot be seen, just as those in seclusion do. HIK's assistant, Sirkar van Stolk, observed this capability in his teacher when he realized that HIK had become part of a larger picture outside his community. "One felt that he was working with the whole of humanity and with every creature on this planet—blessing them, purifying them, raising their vibrations wherever he made contact."[270]

You don't have to be a master to work at this vibrational level, although you probably won't have the range of influence as those more developed beings. During your meditations, you might feel an uplifting connection to all sentient beings or a stream of blissful energy flowing through you. As illustrated in the experiments cited above, some amazing results can also happen with prayer and remote healing.

Many spiritually advanced individuals have such a strong energy field surrounding them that others are stymied by such power. Much as they try, they cannot penetrate it. This story of Umar, Khalif of Arabia, appearing in HIK's *Sufi Tales*, illustrates the effect of this ability.

Someone who wanted to harm Umar was looking for him. He heard that Umar did not live in palaces, though he was a king, but spent most of his time with nature. This man was very glad to think that now he would have every opportunity to accomplish his object. He approached the place where Umar was sitting, but the nearer he came the more his attitude changed; until in the end he dropped the dagger which was in his hand and said, "I cannot harm you. Tell me what is the power in you that keeps me from accomplishing the object which I came to accomplish?" And Umar answered, "My at-one-ment with God."[271]

At a retreat many years ago, I heard a Sufi initiate relate her experience of unexpected power coming from her own energy field. She frequently visited prisoners at a nearby penitentiary, and when one of them was released, he showed up at her house. She offered him coffee and went to the kitchen to make it. Suddenly, she felt uneasy and turned around to find he had a knife and was coming toward her. She held up her hand in defense and to both their astonishment, the knife bent. Completely unhinged, he quickly ran away. I could tell from her demeanor that she spoke the truth and was similarly amazed.

Tenth Oxherding Picture:
Entering the Marketplace with Helping Hands

The gate of his cottage is closed and even the wisest cannot find him. His mental panorama has finally disappeared. He goes his own way, making no attempt to follow the steps of earlier sages. Carrying a gourd, he strolls into the market; leaning on his staff, he returns home. He leads innkeepers and fishmongers in the Way of the Buddha.[272]

The footnote accompanying this commentary of the tenth Oxherding picture states that those in this final stage of the spiritual journey are
so purified, so perfected, that no one, not even the wisest, can detect the
marks of perfection. They no longer appear powerful or elevated. They
no longer exude holiness or any attributes. You may have encountered
individuals who impress you by their spiritual vibration. Perhaps they
look ethereal or have an otherworldly countenance. According to Zen,
these individuals have not reached the final state during which all such
qualities fall away. Those who have reached final enlightenment no
longer have the "stink of holiness." They are outwardly ordinary, but
their effect on the world is extraordinary.

Another footnote to the commentary notes that the gourd he car-
ries is for wine. This means the enlightened one eats and drinks wine
like everyone else. Still, he leads those people around him on the path
to enlightenment. I found this to be true for Adyashanti when I had the
privilege of having dinner with him and a few others when he visited
Ithaca. I could find no air of holiness. He was just an ordinary guy, ordering steak—but no wine—and engaging in casual, fun conversation.

Good works are noble and necessary, but you need to be vigilant that your ego doesn't interfere and take credit for them. Ego can quickly jump in and make you proud of your accomplishments, often in subtle ways. You might feel happy or self-satisfied about what you've achieved, or you might find value in the praise you receive for your actions. There's less danger of this happening when your desire for serving others is so strong that any thought of self disappears. It's also difficult for the ego to intrude if your mere presence has a positive effect on your surroundings without you doing anything. How can you take credit for something you didn't do?

Transforming Presence

The verse following this commentary of the Tenth Oxherding picture underscores how the enlightened Buddha's mere presence transforms his environment.

> Bare-chested, barefooted, he comes into the marketplace.
> Muddied and dust-covered, how broadly he grins!
> Without recourse to mystic powers,
> Withered trees he swiftly brings to bloom.[273]

Like everyone else, the enlightened Buddha goes shopping, but his mere presence, without any effort, profoundly affects his surroundings.

Examples of how a spiritually developed person transforms the environment happens more often than you may realize. I recall a friend telling me that he was in a store with his back to the door looking through the clothing racks. Suddenly, he felt happy, and in turning around saw two Tibetan monks enter the shop. Fr. John, my first spiritual director, would enter a hospital room and the monitors often showed the patient's vitals returning to normal.

Individuals become calmer and more centered when encountering a person who radiates peace, aliveness and truth. Have you ever had this experience in which you felt better, or your life got better, when a certain person came into your life, even though they didn't "do" anything? Perhaps you are or were that person for someone else.

Influence

There is a story about a poor man whose job was to sell empty bottles in Bombay. He came to a merchant and asked a certain salary to do this work for him, and from the day the merchant engaged him he steadily became more prosperous. So, one day he thought, "I have worked for twenty years in this shop, and it is only since this young man has come that I have prospered." He did not tell this to the young man, but the next day he made him a partner in his business; and from that time, he began to flourish a hundred times more. After six months he was flourishing and prospering in every way, and in the end, as he had no children, he gave his business to this young man, who in time became the wealthiest man in the whole country.[274]

–Khan, *Tales*

Enlightened masters have an even greater positive influence on all who surround them. I'm struck by the similar descriptions given by Buddhist Richard Baker and Sufi Sirkar van Stolk of their respective teachers, Shunryu Suzuki and HIK. Baker writes:

Without anything said or done, just the impact of meeting a personality so developed can be enough to change another's whole way of life. But in the end, it is not the extraordinariness of the teacher which perplexes, intrigues and deepens the student, it is the teacher's utter ordinariness. Because he is just himself, he is a mirror for his students. When we are with him, we feel our own strengths and shortcomings without any sense of praise or criticism from him. In his presence we see our original face, and the extraordinariness we see is only our own true nature.[275]

Here, the themes of ordinary/extraordinary and transformation of others by a mystic's presence arise again. Sikhar van Stolk's impression of HIK in *Memories of a Sufi Sage* also shows the astonishing effect the mere presence of a realized being has on the world.

The great Initiate is nothing in himself; something shines through him. By contact with him the ordinary person receives glimpses of something far greater than his or her own self, something so fine, beautiful and steadfast that it is breathtaking. The Initiate dispenses spiritual sustenance to starving souls in much the same way as a lighthouse pours its radiance upon a dark world. He himself is so immersed in the "Divine Realities" that he radiates love, harmony and beauty at every breath. To those who are even a little open to these mysteries, the presence of such a soul is in itself a revelation.[276]

Somehow, the students of these great masters are spiritually changed by just being in their presence. This may inspire you to develop sufficiently so that, without any doing on your part, your presence helps uplift others.

Your Light in the World

How does your spiritual growth affect the world? You might share an inspiring book, blog or teaching video with a friend. You might show kindness and compassion to someone undergoing a difficult time. You might bring food to someone who is ill or share a funny story with someone who is sad. Your profession may help or inspire others. You might join together with others to effect social, environmental, political or spiritual change. During meditation, you might sense you're connecting with others all over the planet and feel all of you together are having a positive impact on the world. Just your presence might help others relax and feel at peace.

Hasidic Judaism claims that even the simplest everyday activities performed in holiness can give rise to the upliftment of the world. Practicing in this way, you become a channel uniting heaven and earth, the Divine and human, the upper and lower worlds.

He who prays and sings in holiness, eats and speaks in holiness, in holiness takes the prescribed ritual bath and in holiness is mindful of his business, through him the fallen sparks are raised and the fallen worlds redeemed and renewed.[277]

I'm sure at times you felt separated from your True Nature, from the Radiant All. Hasidism shows you a way to consciously regain that connection by being aware of the sacredness and meaningfulness of all your actions.

Wouldn't it be amazing if you could view all your actions as a sacred ritual? You would have to slow down, since rituals are about the present moment, not getting to the end. You would have to practice mindfulness—being in the present moment with total concentration. You wouldn't care about the results because that would be a future activity. If you viewed all actions as sacred you would become an increasing light in the world, uplifting all those around you.

Global Transformation

With the power of the internet, opportunities for individuals to join together for the upliftment of the planet have increased exponentially. Consciousness about global warming, the intense suffering of so many people across the world, the extinction of many species, and the myriad of injustices plaguing our society cry out for change. Yes, the mystics have created important social change stemming from their presence and action, but a confluence of many seekers to address and reform these conditions is sorely needed now more than ever. This could take an interior form of thousands of people praying together at a selected day and time, or it could take an exterior action in the form of emails, marches, protests or work for like-minded organizations. Seekers following the feminine way in particular understand that the contemplative life and social and environmental action are two necessary facets of the same path.[278]

I belong to a Sufi Healing Group that prays weekly on Zoom for the people who need healing—whether in their body, heart or soul—and for the planet. The opening prayer is said in several languages and the presenters from various parts of the world take turns leading. I often feel a great wave of energy surrounding the planet as we pray. The TM experiment cited above cogently illustrates the effect such a group can have on the environment.

Spiritual growth is effusive. It's always accompanied by some effect on the world, whether you engage in some kind of activity, work vibrationally through prayer and meditation, or change your environment by your mere presence. Mystics from both the East and West are the luminaries in these areas. Their impact is world-wide and long-lasting. It extends beyond life on earth to unknown worlds. Your own spiritual development and groups coming together in prayer or action also powerfully benefit the world. I hope the examples cited in this chapter inspire you as they have me.

Reflections on Becoming a Light in the World

1. What would it be like to see each moment as holy?

2. Have you had experiences of the effectiveness of remote prayer and meditation?

3. What kind of presence would you like to be in the world?

4. Imagine healing energy flowing through and radiating from your breath, heart, hands and speech.

Chapter 14:
The Dance

Dance, dervish, dance
Bring the Face of God before you.

Only Love can lift the heart up so high
That its true Color is restored by the Sun!
See Him near and clapping,
That Perfect One who fathers Divine Rhythm.

O dance, dervish dance,
And know you bring your Master happiness
Whenever you smile.[279]

–Hafiz

The spiritual journey is a captivating dance. It doesn't matter when you become aware of the dance, when you take your first step or when you realize it's a life-long work in progress. What matters is the dance itself. How can you gracefully move and flow through the intricacies of the dance at any moment in time? How can you live a life of love, harmony and beauty as Hazrat Inayat Khan suggests? How can you continue with the dance when you feel you've lost your way?

In reading *Dance of Light*, you may have become inspired by the depth and richness of the spiritual life. You may have devoured all that is written, wanting to know more, or found yourself disagreeing with some of the ideas. Alternatively, you may have become discouraged, thinking you will never be able to experience the sublime heights of the illuminative or unitive states. Again, it doesn't matter.

What's important is to realize the preciousness of your being and enjoy the dance of the present moment without worrying about your place on the dance floor.

As indicated in *Dance of Light*, the spiritual journey helps you become more fully conscious of your True Nature and your connection with the preciousness of all life. Perhaps you now understand the purpose of some of your life's difficulties (purification) and what parts of your life need stripping away or transforming. You may see the value of having a guide or being in a place of unknowing. You may now recognize what pitfalls to avoid, such as putting too much emphasis on spiritual highs, becoming too attached to your self-identities, or believing the narratives you created about your life. Hopefully you have learned how to work with distractions and realize what transformation techniques are available for you. You may now have more self-acceptance of your own experience of the dance, not trying to slow it down or speed it up.

For a brief time, we have danced this dance together. May your life's journey continue to unfold in wondrous ways! May you become a radiant light in the world.

Endnotes

1   Evelyn Underhill, *Mysticism: A Study in the Nature and Development of Man's Spiritual Consciousness* (New York: E.P. Dutton, 1961).

2   Wim Van Den Dungen, *Ten Ox-Herding Images: Training the Mind for Enlightenment* (Brasschaat, Belgium: Taurus Press, 2018).

3   Three of these stages—Purgation or Purification (of the self), Illumination and Union—date back to the early Church Fathers and are often featured in the mystical writings in both Eastern Orthodox and Western Christianity. John of the Cross in the sixteenth century focused on a part of the journey that was previously not separated out and called it the Dark Night of the Soul. This is logically placed between the Illuminative and Unitive states. Evelyn Underhill in *Mysticism* (New York: E.P. Dutton, 1961) adds the Awakening Stage and succeeds in explaining these stages in great detail. I have added two preliminary stages, titled The Dark Wood and Finding Your Way, which parallel the first two stages in the Zen Oxherding Pictures. The title of the final stage, *Entering the Marketplace with Helping Hands*, is taken from the Zen tradition, although the idea is implied in all the traditions. This portrays the impact the journeyer has in the world.

4   Martine Batchelor, "The Ten Oxherding Pictures," *Tricycle* (Spring 2000). https://tricycle.org/magazine/ten-oxherding-pictures/. This series of ten drawings with commentary attributed to Kakuan Shien, a Chinese Zen master of the twelfth century, is based on even earlier Buddhist teachings. If you contemplate each phrase of these poetic teachings and allow them to resonate within the deepest part of your being, your understanding of the path will become clear. Ching-chu of the eleventh century had a series of five images, with the Ox gradually getting whiter until it disappeared. Jitoku Zenji (1090–1159) worked with six pictures. I love how the Oxherding pictures evolved in a similar way to the Christian tradition's stages, as noted by Underhill.

5   Eva de Vitray-Meyerovitch, *Rumi and Sufism,* trans. Simone Fattal (Sausalito, CA: The Post-Apollo Press, 1987), 93-4.

6   For example, the Genesis story of Adam and Eve eating from the tree of good and evil symbolizes the concept duality, which brings suffering into the world. This is similar to the Four Noble Truths of Buddhism which says suffering is the result of ego desires, which separates the individual from the whole and ushers in duality.

7   John of the Cross, *Dark Night of the Soul* (Garden City, NY: Doubleday, 1959), 33-34.

8   Meister Eckhart in Sermon 83 talks about the namelessness of God and our inability to attribute proper and clearly defined names to God. *Meister Eckhart, The Essential Sermons, Commentaries, Treatises and Defense,* trans. and ed. Bernard McGinn and Edmund Colledge (New York: Paulist Press, 1981).

9   Augustine Thompson, O. P. *Francis of Assisi: A New Biography* (Ithaca, NY: Cornell University Press, 2012).

10   Pierre Teilhard de Chardin, *Hymn of the Universe* (New York: Harper & Row, 1965), 59-71.

11   Matthew Fox, *Illuminations of Hildegard of Bingen* (Rochester, VT: Bear & Company, 2003).

12   Mirabai Starr, *Wild Mercy: Living the Fierce and Tender Wisdom of the Women Mystics* (Boulder, CO: Sounds True, 2019).

13   Cynthia Bourgeault, *Eye of the Heart: A Spiritual Journey into the Imaginal Realm* (Boulder, CO: Shambhala Publications, 2020).

14   Paul Brunton, *The Notebooks of Paul Brunton: Perspectives* (Burdett, NY: Larson Publications, 1984), 313.

15   Beverly Lanzetta, *The Monk Within: Embracing the Sacred Way of Life* (Sebastopol, CA: Blue Sapphire Books, 2018), 91-103.

16   The feminine way generally views spirituality from a more bodily and worldly perspective. It sees the goal as dwelling within rather than beyond you. Meditations are geared toward taking you deeper into your own mind-body-soul system. The feminine way also places more emphasis on relatedness/sexuality, social/political action, and growth through the natural world and community.

17   Hazrat Inayat Khan, *The Alchemy of Happiness* (London: East-West Publications, 1996) 271.

18   Ekai Kawaguchi as quoted in Paul Reps and Nyogen Senzaki, *Zen Flesh, Zen Bones: A Collection of Zen and Pre-Zen Writings* (Rutledge, VT: Tuttle Publishing, 1985, c. 1957), 175.

19   Adyashanti, "The Great Expense of Darkness," May 2019, Granli-bakken Tahoe, 1 hr. 4 min., *Silent Retreat Vol. 72 Talks*, CD or MP3, https://www.adyashanti.org/store/media/audio-downloads/1085.

20   Hinduism focuses on reaching samadhi—a totally out-of-body experience, during which the guru is no longer conscious of the world. There's less emphasis on the guru coming back into the world to transform his disciples and elevate his surroundings, even though this occurs. The teachings of Christianity, Judaism and Sufism focus on bringing the spiritual into everyday life.

21   Rabbi Susya as quoted in Martin Buber, *Hasidism and Modern Man* (Atlantic Highlands, NJ: Humanities Press International, 1988), 132.

22   *The Bhagavad Gita* trans. Swami Prabhabananda and Frederick A. Manchester (New York, NY: Penguin Books, 1979), 59.

23   Hazrat Inayat Khan, *The Complete Works of Pir-O-Murshid Hazrat Inayat Khan, Lectures on Sufism 1924 II: June 10-End of December* (New Lebanon, NY: Omega Publications, 2009) 517-8.

24   Dante Alighieri, *The Divine Comedy: The Inferno, The Purgatorio, The Paradiso*, trans. John Cardi (New York, NY: New American Library, 2003), 16.

25   Philip Kapleau, *Three Pillars of Zen* (Boston: Beacon Press, 1967), 302.

26   Kapleau, 302.

27   This is the title of her book. Jess Lair, *I Don't Know Where I'm Going, But I Sure Ain't Lost* (Robbinsdale, MN: Fawcett Publications, 1983).

28   Kapleau, 303.

29   Fr. S. J. George Maloney (1924–2005) wrote many books on spirituality such as *Prayer of the Heart, The Everlasting Now,* and *Called to Intimacy.*

30   Fr. Thomas Berry (1914–2009) was a Passionist priest, a leading cultural historian, and a pioneer in the field of ecology and spirituality. He wrote such books as *The Dream of the Earth* and *The Sacred Universe.*

31   Hafiz. *I Heard God Laughing: Renderings of Hafiz*, trans. Daniel Ladinsky (Walnut Creek, CA: Sufism Reoriented, 1996), 27.

32   Linda Sabbath, *The Radiant Heart* (Denville, NJ: Dimension Books, 1977).

33   Paramahansa Yogananda, *Autobiography of a Yogi* (Los Angeles, Self-Realization Fellowship, 1977), 106.

34   Yogananda, 107.

35   Tagore quoted in F.C. Happold, *Mysticism: A Study and an Anthology* (Middlesex, England, Penguin Books, 1963), p. 140.

36   Adyashanti, *The End of Your World: Uncensored Straight Talk on the Nature of Enlightenment* (Boulder, CO: Sounds True, 2008) 129-158.

37   Adyashanti, *The End of Your World*, 18.

38   Acts 9:3-4, 7-9 in *The Jerusalem Bible*, trans. Alexander Jones (Garden City, NY: Doubleday, 1967), 214-15.

39   Pir Vilayat Inayat Khan, *Call of the Dervish* (Santa Fe, NM: Sufi Order Publications, 1981), 37.

40   Sherry Ruth Anderson and Patricia Hopkins, *The Feminine Face of God: The Unfolding of the Sacred in Women* (New York, NY: Bantam Book, 1991), 13-14.

41   Adyashanti, *End of Your World*, 129-58.

42   R. C. Bucke, *Cosmic Consciousness: A Study in the Evolution of the Human Mind,* as quoted in F.C. Happold, 136.

43   Hazrat Inayat Khan, *Gayan, Vadan, Nirtan* (Lebanon Springs, NY: Sufi Order Publications, 1980), 106.

44   Khan, *Gayan*, 98.

45   Kapleau, 304.

46   Russell Heimlich, "Mystical Experiences," Pew Research Center Fact-Tank, December 29, 2009, https://www.pewresearch.org/fact-tank/2009/12/29/mystical-experiences/.

47   Adyashanti, *Emptiness Dancing* (Boulder, CO: Sounds True, 2006), 138.

48   Starr, 62.

49   Kapleau, 302.

50   The term purification goes as far back as the fourth century in the writings of Gregory of Nyssa. *Gregory of Nyssa: The Life of Moses*, trans. Everett Ferguson and Abraham J. Malherbe (New York: Paulist Press, 1978). Self-simplification is a term coined by Richard of St. Victor (d. 1173), according to Underhill, 204.

51   Martin Prechtel, *Secrets of the Talking Jaguar* (New York, NY: Tarcher/Putnam, 1998), 33.

52   Khan, *The Gathas* (1982), 239.

53   The term purification goes as far back as the fourth century in the writings of Gregory of Nyssa. *Gregory of Nyssa: The Life of Moses*, trans. Everett Ferguson and Abraham J. Malherbe (New York: Paulist Press, 1978). Self-simpli-

fication is a term coined by Richard of St. Victor (d. 1173), according to Underhill, 204.

54   Cantos X-XII of the Purgatorio in Dante's *Divine Comedy* includes the need to let go of pride so as to become humble.

55   Attar's poem, "The Conference of the Birds," quoted in Pir Zia Inayat Khan *Mingled Waters: Sufism and the Mystical Unity of Religions* (New Lebanon, NY: Suluk Press, 2017) 226.

56   Kapleau, 305-306.

57   Muso Soseki, *Dialogues in a Dream: The Life and Zen Teaching of Muso Soseki,* trans. Thomas Yuho Kirchner (Sommerville, MA: Wisdom Publications, 2015).

58   Anandamayi Ma, *Sri Anandamayi Ma Quotes and Teachings: A collection of 108 Quotes of Sri Anandamayi Ma,* https://www.hindu-blog.com/2018/09/sri-anandamayi-ma-quotes-and-teachings.html.

59   Amoda Maa, retreat at Treman Center, Ithaca, NY, April 27-28, 2019.

60   John Reps and Nyogen Senzaki, *Zen Flesh, Zen Bones: A Collection of Zen and Pre-Zen Writings* (Rutledge, VT: Tuttle Publications, 1985, c. 1957), 164-5.

61   Adyashanti said this at various retreats at Omega Institute from September 2008-2011.

62   This verse in the poem "Mathnawi" by Rumi is excerpted in Andrew Harvey (Editor) *Teachings of Rumi,* Boulder, CO: Shambhala Publications, 1999, 3.

63   Thomas Merton, *New Seeds of Contemplation* (New York, NY: New Directions, 1972), 203.

64   Underhill, 230.

65   A common practice in the Inayati Sufi Order.

66   Hakim Jami as quoted in Idries Shah, *The Way of the Sufi* (New York, NY: E.P. Dutton, 1970) 140.

67   C. J. Jung, *Memories, Dreams, and Reflections* (New York: Vintage Books, 1965), 290-1.

68   Teilhard de Chardin, 66.

69   Starr, 193.

70   Starr, 195.

71   This quote is by Gelac Peterson, written in 1616, as quoted in Underhill, 212.

72   Jean M. Twenge, A. Bell Cooper, Thomas E. Joiner, and Mary E. Duffy, "Age, Period, and Cohort Trends in Mood Disorder Indicators and Suicide-Related

outcomes in a Nationally Representative Dataset, 2005-2017," *Journal of Abnormal Psychology* 128, no. 3, (2019): 185-199. http://dx.doi.org/10.1037/abn0000410. Elizabeth M. Seabrook, Margaret L. Kern, Nikki S. Rickard, "Social Networking Sites, Depression, and Anxiety: A Systematic Review," *JMIR Mental Health* 3, no. 4 (2016): e50. https://mental.jmir.org/2016/4/e50.

73   Attributed to Bokuju.

74   Adyashanti, *Emptiness Dancing* (Boulder, CO: Sounds True, 2006), 76.

75   Thomas Merton, *The Way of Chuang Tzu*, (Boulder, CO: Shambhala, 2004), 122.

76   *The Bhagavad Gita*, 2:47, 52.

77   Rabbi Susya as quoted in Buber, p. 132.

78   Reps and Senzaki, *Zen Flesh, Zen Bones*, 101-2.

79   Scott Peck, *The Road Less Traveled* (New York, Simon & Schuster, 1978), 187–191.

80   Alfred North Whitehead, *Science and the Modern World* (New York, NY: Free Press, 1977 c. 1925), 58.

81   Howard Thurman, "The Sound of the Genuine," March 12, 1980, *Expanding Common Ground: The Howard Thurman & Sue Bailey Thurman Collections at Boston University*, 41:53, http://archives.bu.edu/web/howard-thurman/virtual-listening-room/detail?id=360318.

82   Reps and Senzaki, 102-3.

83   John of the Cross, *Ascent of Mount Carmel* (Garden City, NY: Doubleday Image, 1958), 156.

84   Khan, *Gayan*, 62.

85   Hazrat Inayat Khan, *Mastery Through Accomplishment* (New Lebanon, NY, Omega Press, 1978), 147–155.

86   Amoda Maa, *Falling Open in a World Falling Apart: The Essential Teaching Amoda Maa* (Burdett, NY: Larson Publications, 2020), 47.

87   *Julian of Norwich: Showings,* trans. Edmund Colledge, O.S.A. and James Walsh, S.J. (New York, NY: Paulist Press, 1978), 225. Julian of Norwich wrote the best-known surviving book in the English language by a mystic and the first book written in English by a woman.

88   Meister Eckhart as quoted in Underhill, 209.

89   Adyashanti, *Falling into Grace* (Boulder, CO, Sounds True, 2011), 37–44.

90   Matthew 21:12-37, *The Jerusalem Bible*, 48.

91   Johannes Tauler as quoted in *Teachings of the Christian Mystics* edited by Andrew Harvey (Boulder, CO: Shambhala, 2019), 96.

92 Maa, 39.

93 Attributed to Ram Dass.

94 "Love and do what you will" is a modernized phrasing to a passage in Saint Augustine's Seventh Homily on 1 John 4:4-12 as quoted in Underhill, 216.

95 Gandhi was quoting from Swami Prabhavananda and Frederick A. Manchester, *The Upanishads: Breadth of the Eternal: The Principal Texts* (New York, NY: New American Library, 1957), 27-8.

96 John Mark Green, *Johnmarkgreenpoetry.tumblr.com,* Nov. 8, 2015, https://johnmarkgreenpoetry.tumblr.com/post/132839955315/beautiful-are-those-whose-brokenness-gives-birth.

97 Underhill, 220.

98 Kapleau, 305.

99 Kapleau, 305

100 Kapleau, 306.

101 Khan, *The Complete Works,* 210–11.

102 Matthew Fox, *Meditations with Meister Eckhart* (Rochester, NY: Bear & Company, 1983), 58.

103 John McBride is quoted by Nick Paumgarten in "The Descent of Man," *The New Yorker* (April 28, 2019).

104 Theophane the Monk, *Tales of the Magic Monastery* (Reno, NV: Crossroad, 2010), 50.

105 Lama Tsultrum Allione, *Feeding Your Demons: Ancient Wisdom for Resolving Inner Conflict* (New York, NY: Little, Brown Spark, 2008).

106 Margaret Mitchell as quoted in Anderson & Hopkins, 124.

107 Khan, *The Gathas,* 147.

108 This Sufi tale appears in Hazrat Inayat Kahn, *Tales* (New Lebanon, NY: Omega Press, 1980), 164.

109 Robert A. Johnson, *Inner Work: Using Dreams and Imagination for Personal Growth* (San Francisco, CA: Harper & Row, 1986).

110 See, for example, Anodea Judith, *Eastern Body, Western Mind: Psychology and the Chakra System as a Path to the Self* (Berkley, CA: Celestial Arts, 1996).

111 Sabbath, 39.

112 John 4:13-14, *The Jerusalem Bible,* 152-3.

113 Peter Levine, *Waking the Tiger: Healing Trauma* (Berkeley, CA: North Atlantic Books, 1997).

114 David Berceli, *Trauma Releasing Exercises: A Revolutionary New*

Method for Stress/Trauma Recovery (Charleston, SC: Book Surge Publishing, 2005) 60.

115 Bessel van der Kolk, M.D., *The Body Keeps the Score* (New York, NY: Penguin Books, 2014).

116 Wilhelm Reich, *Character Analysis*, translated by Theodore P. Wolfe (New York, NY: Farrar & Straus, 1971). Reich's work, originally published in German in 1933, was the basis for bioenergetic psychotherapy. Alexander Lowen, *The Language of the* Body (New York, NY: Collier, 1971. John Pierrakos, *Core Energetics: Developing the Capacity to Love and Heal* (Mendocino, CA: Life Rhythms Publications, 1990.

117 Alice McDowell, *Hidden Treasure: How to Break Free of Five Patterns that Hide Your True Self* (Berkeley, CA: She Writes Press, 2017).

118 Hafiz, "Tired of Speaking Sweetly," *The Gift: Poems of Hafiz,* trans. Daniel Ladinsky (New York, NY: Arkana, 1999), 187-8.

119 Hazrat Inayat Khan, *The Heart of Sufism* (Boston: Shambala Press, 1999), 286.

120 Camile and Kabir Helminsky, *Rumi Daylight: A Daybook of Spiritual Guidance* (Putney, VT: Threshold Books, 1990), 39.

121 Sai Baba is said to have described marriage this way to one of his devotees and it has been attributed to her.

122 Theophane the Monk, 68.

123 Anderson and Hopkins, 184.

124 As quoted in McDowell, *Hidden Treasure*, 156.

125 Jerry Seinfeld as quoted in "Everything You Need to know About Parenting from 8 Jerry Seinfeld Quotes," *Fatherly.com*, June 4, 2015. https://www.fatherly.com/love-money/everything-you-need-to-know-about-parenting-from-8-jerry-seinfeld-quotes/.

126 Paramahansa Yogananda quoting Anandamayi Ma, *Autobiography of a Yogi*, 524.

127 Huston Smith, *The World Religions: Our Great Wisdom Traditions* (San Francisco, HarperCollins, 1991), 50-54.

128 Smith, 50-55.

129 Hafiz, *The Subject Tonight is Love: 60 Wild and Sweet Poems*, trans. Daniel Ladinsky (Los Angeles: Pumpkin House Press, 1996), 13.

130 I believe blessings are showered upon us at all times, but busyness, distractions, social obligations and selfish concerns deflect them like an umbrella.

Letting go of these distractions, whether actively or passively, allows you to lower the umbrella and receive the gifts.

131 The four empires which collapsed are the German Empire, The Hapsburgs, The Ottoman Empire and The Romanov Empire.

132 Hazrat Inayat Khan, *The Complete Sayings of Hazrat Inayat Khan* (New Lebanon, NY: Sufi Order Publications, 1978), 229.

133 Teresa of Ávila, *Book of the Foundations,* trans. Rev. John Dalton (London: T. Jones, 1853), 27.

134 Adyashanti, *The End of Your World*, 29.

135 John of the Cross, *Living Flame of Love* (Garden City, NY: Image Books, 1962), 41.

136 Smith, 33.

137 Khan, *Gayan*, 177.

138 Song of Songs 1:1, *The Jerusalem Bible,* 993.

139 Proverbs 8:17, *The Jerusalem Bible*, 942.

140 Alexander Jones, *The Jerusalem Bible: The New Testament* (Garden City, NY: Doubleday, 1967), Volume 2:180.

141 Smith, 34.

142 *The Bhagavad Gita*, 11:53-4, 95.

143 Elisabeth Kübler-Ross quoted in Anne Nietzke, "The Miracle of Elisabeth Kübler-Ross," *Cosmopolitan* (February 1980), 211.

144 Hafiz, *The Gift*, 40.

145 Kapleau, 307.

146 Prabhavananda and Manchester, *The Upanishads*, 69.

147 Kapleau, 308.

148 Alice McDowell, "Altered States of Consciousness and Mystical Experience: A Topology of Inner Space" (doctoral thesis, Fordham University, 1971), 81.

149 Anne Bancroft, *Weavers of Wisdom: Women Mystics of the Twentieth Century* (London: Arkana, 1989), 76-77.

150 Meister Eckhart as quoted in Fox, 14.

151 Attributed to Zen Buddhist Layman P'ang Yün (740-808) as quoted in Daisetz T. Suzuki, *Japanese and Zen Culture* (New York, NY: Bollingen Foundation, 1959), 16.

152 Sirkar van Stolk and Daphne Dunlop, *Memories of a Sufi Sage: Hazrat Inayat Khan* (The Hague: East-West Publications Fonds B.V., 1967), 111-113.

153 St. Bernard of Clairvaux is quoted in Alfred Wautier d'Aygalliers, Fred

Rothwell, *Ruysbroeck the Admirable* (London: J.M. Dent & Sons, 1925), 232.

154 Annie Dillard, *Pilgrim at Tinker Creek* (New York: Harper's Magazine Press, 1974).

155 Daniel 6:17–25. *The Jerusalem Bible*, 1436.

156 Kapleau, 312.

157 Underhill, 260.

158 Paul Hawken, *The Magic of Findhorn* (New York: Harper and Row, 1975).

159 Crombie's explanation is cited in Hawken, 142-3.

160 John 1:9, *The Holy Bible* (RSV) (New York, NY: New American Library, 1962), 86.

161 Dante, *The Divine Comedy*, Paradiso, XXX, 97-99, 863.

162 *The Flower Ornament Scripture*, trans. Thomas Leary (Boulder, CO: Shambala Publications, 1993), 149.

163 Khan, 248.

164 *The Bhagavad Gita*, 11:12, 90.

165 Anderson and Hopkins, 169.

166 Aldous Huxley, "Visionary Experience," in John White, editor, The *Highest State of Consciousness* (Garden City, NY: Anchor Books, 1972), 49.

167 Huxley in White, 35-37.

168 Raymond Mooney, *Life After Life* (New York, NY: Bantam Books, 1976), 58.

169 Lucy Menzies, *The Revelations of Mechthild of Magdeburg* (London: Longmans, Green & Co., 1953), 194.

170 Dante, *The Divine Comedy*, Paradiso, XXX, 61, 863.

171 McDowell, "Altered States of Consciousness and Mystical Experience," 108.

172 Underhill, 344.

173 Ruysbroeck as quoted in Underhill, 235.

174 Hafiz, *I Heard God Laughing*, 1.

175 Exodus 34:29, *The Holy Bible: Old Testament* (RSV), 80.

176 Matthew 17:1–2 *The Holy Bible: New Testament* (RSV), 18.

177 Mircea Eliade, *The Two and the One* (New York, NY: Harper Torchbooks, 1969), 64.

178 Eliade, 64.

179 Attributed to St. Basil the Great.

180 Hafiz, *The Gift*, 199.

181 Pir Valayat Khan, *The Message in Our Time: The Life and Teachings of Pir-O-Murshid Inayat Khan* (San Francisco, CA: Harper & Row, 1979), 11.

182 Smith, 197.

183 Underhill, 257.

184 Raymond Moody, *Reflections on Life After Life* (New York: Bantam Books, 1977).

185 Moody, 10-11.

186 Lina Eckenstein, *Woman Under Monasticism* (Cambridge: Cambridge University Press, 1896), 275.

187 Underhill, 281-290.

188 John of the Cross, *Spiritual Canticle* (Garden City, NY: Doubleday Image, 1961), 320.

189 These can be found in the writings of Julian of Norwich, Catherine of Siena, Teresa of Ávila, Johannes Tauler and Henry Suso as discussed in Underhill, 398.

190 In another so-called lower form of channeling, the words come through the channeler's mouth directly without any consciousness of what these words are until they emerge. See Corrine McLaughlin, "Tuning into the Best Channel," *New Realities*, July/August 1987, 41.

191 Theophane the Monk, 92.

192 Bob L. "The Second Step," *Mysterious Ways,* Aug/Sept 2019, 29.

193 Adyashanti, *The End of Your World*, 117-128.

194 You can see this for yourself on YouTube: https://www.youtube.com/watch?v=ZXqBg1Uirbo.

195 John 6:1-15, *The Jerusalem Bible*, 157.

196 *Seeing is Believing,* Season 1, Episode 1, "Pray, Hope and Don't Worry: A Celebration of Padre Pio," directed by J. Paddy Nolan, aired in 1989, JPN Film Services Production.

197 Kennedy, Daniel Joseph, "St. Thomas Aquinas," in Herbermann, Charles (ed.). *Catholic Encyclopedia* 14 (New York: Robert Appleton Company, 1912).

198 Yogananda.

199 Nagarjuna: *The Treatise on the Great Perfection of Wisdom* http://the-wanderling.com/siddhis.html.

200 Takao Mauryani, "Buddha's Supernatural Powers in the Lotus Sutra," https://core.ac.uk/download/pdf/148766201.pdf.

201 Zen master Yasutani quoted in Kapleau, 40-41.

202 Helen Bacovcin, *The Way of a Pilgrim; And the Pilgrim Continues His Way: A New Translation* (Garden City, NY: Image Books, 1978), 167.

203 Jack Kornfield, *A Path with a Heart* (New York, NY: Bantam Books, 1993), 129.

204 Kapleau, 41.

205 Kornfield, 129.

206 Pir Vilayat Inayat Khan, *Thinking Like the Universe: The Sufi Path of Awakening,* reprint edition, ed. Pythia Peay (New York, NY: Thorsons, 2000), 183.

207 Some of these attachments were described centuries ago by John of the Cross in his book, *Dark Night of the Soul*, and they still have relevance today. See John of the Cross, *Dark Night of the Soul*, 39-42.

208 Adyashanti, *The End of Your World*, 196.

209 Jack Kornfield, 150.

210 Carlos Castaneda, *The Eagle's Gift*, (New York, NY: Simon & Schuster, 1981), 224.

211 St. Thérèse of Lisieux. *The Story of a Soul* (Charlotte, NC: TAN Books, 2010), 120-121.

212 Gerald Brennan, *St. John of the Cross: His Life and Poetry* (Cambridge, MA: Cambridge University Press, 1973), 30-32.

213 *The Life of St. Teresa of Ávila*, trans. Alice Lady Lovat (London: Herbert & Daniel, 1912), 548.

214 John of the Cross, *Dark Night of the* Soul, 154.

215 The Oxherding pictures do not include a separate entry for the Dark Night of the Soul. Interestingly, the Christian tradition did not separate out the Dark Night in describing the spiritual stages until the sixteenth century when John of the Cross formally introduced the concept.

216 Kapleau, 308.

217 van Stolk and Dunlop, 80-81.

218 Timothy Freke, *The Wisdom of the Christian Mystics* (Boston, MA: Godsfield Press, 1998), 24.

219 John of the Cross, *Spiritual Canticle*, 180-181.

220 Adyashanti, *The End of Your World*, 165-174.

221 Adyashanti, 197.

222 Gangaji and Roslyn Moore, *Just Like You* (Mendocino, CA: Do Pub, 2003) 157.

223 Anthony DeMello, https://www.demellospirituality.com/freedom/the-harder-you-try-to-change-the-worse-it-get/

224 *Julian of Norwich*, 225.

225 Adyashanti, *The End of Your World*, 173.

226 Adyashanti, 169.

227 Layman P'ang, *The Sayings of Layman P'ang: A Zen Classic of China*, trans. James Green (Boulder, CO: Shambhala Publications, 2009) 15.

228 Gangaji and Moore, 137.

229 Gangaji and Moore, 174.

230 Kapleau, 309.

231 Kapleau, 310.

232 Pema Chödrön, *Welcoming the Unwelcome: Wholehearted Living in a Brokenhearted World* (Boulder, CO: Shambhala, 2019), 38.

233 Richard Baker in the Introduction to *Zen Mind, Beginner's Mind* by Suzuki, Shunryu and Trudy Dixon (New York: Weatherhill, 1980), 18.

234 Meister Eckhart as quoted in Freke, *Wisdom of the Christian Mystics*, 25.

235 John of the Cross, *Dark Night of the Soul*, 33-34.

236 John of the Cross, *Living Flame of Love*, 79.

237 Marguerite Porete falls into this camp. "The liberated soul loses her name in the One through Whom and in Whom she merges; just as a river reaching the sea loses the identity with which it flowed through many countries to arrive at the sea." In Freke, *Christian Mystics*, 19.

238 Richard of St. Victor illustrates the second view of the continual existence of the soul, transformed. "When a soul is plunged in the fire of divine love, like iron, it loses its blackness, and in the fire of divine love, like iron, it becomes like unto fire itself. And lastly, it grows liquid and losing its nature is transmuted into an utterly different quality of being," as quoted in Underhill, 421.

239 H. A. Reinhold, ed., *The Soul Afire: Revelations of the Mystics* (New York, NY: Meridian Books, 1960), 300-301.

240 Reinhold, 301.

241 John of the Cross, *Spiritual Canticle*, 464.

242 Khan, *The Complete Sayings*, 60.

243 Hafiz, *The Gift*, 84.

244 Timothy Freke, *The Wisdom of the Sufi Sages* (Boston, MA: Godsfield Press, 1999), 54.

245 Practitioners of zikr also recite three derivative phrases from the full statement. The first, "illa 'llah hu" means "but God" or rather "only God." Repeating "only God" over and over again brings the seeker closer to that oneness. The second derivative phrase, "Allah hu" means "God, just He" or "God, just She" or "God, just It." I love that "hu" is genderless. Again, this points toward oneness— just God and nothing else. The third phrase, "hu," which is closest in meaning to "om," the original sound of the universe, is whispered deep within, brings the practitioner even closer to Divine consciousness.

246 Qur'an 2:115. A. Helwa, *Secrets of Divine Love: A Spiritual Journey into the Heart of Islam* (Capistrano Beach, CA: Naulit Publishing House, 2020) cited this passage on page 26 from Yahiya Emerick's translation, *The Holy Qur'an in Today's English*, self-published 2010.

247 "Love is to stand before your Beloved/stripped naked of all attributes/so that His qualities become your qualities," al-Hallaj as quoted in Freke, *The Wisdom of the Sufi Sages*, 55.

248 Ibn 'Arabi as quoted in Freke, *The Wisdom of the Sufi Sages*, 40.

249 van Stock and Dunlop, 75-76.

250 Gangaji and Moore, 157-8.

251 Gangaji and Moore, 138.

252 M. O'C. Walsh, trans. and ed., *Meister Eckhart: Sermons and Treatises*, Vol. 3 (Rockport, MA: Element Books, 1979) as quoted in Harvey, 89.

253 Dionysius the Aeropagite as quoted in Happold, 191.

254 Adyashanti, *Emptiness Dancing*, 151.

255 Yaqin Aubert, Esoteric Secretary for Pir Zia Inayat Khan, *The Lataif with Naima Brown and Yaqin Aubert*, webinar, April 27, 2021.

256 Red Pine, trans., *The Heart Sutra* (Berkley, CA: Counterpoint Press, 2004), 158.

257 Lao Tsu, Gia-Fu Feng and Jane English. *Tao Te Ching* (New York, NY: Vintage Books, 1972), Chapter 14.

258 McDowell, "Altered States of Consciousness and Mystical Experience," 160.

259 McDowell, 111.

260 Eben Alexander, *Proof of Heaven: A Neurosurgeon's Journey into the Afterlife* (New York: Simon & Schuster, 2012), 46-8.

261 Abu sa'id ibn Abi-L-Khayr as quoted in Freke, *The Wisdom of the Sufi Sages*, 37.

262 J. S. Hagelin, D. W. Orme-Johnson, M. Rainforth, K. Cavanaugh, C. N. Alexander, S. F. Shatkin, J. L. Davies, A. O. Hughs and E. Ross, "Effects of Group Practice of the Transcendental Meditation Program on Preventing Violent Crime in Washington, D.C.: Results of the National Demonstration Project, June-July 1993," *Social Indicators Research* 47, no. 2:153-201. Michael C. Dillbeck and Kenneth L. Cavanaugh, "Societal Violence and Collective Consciousness: Reduction of U.S. Homicide and Urban Violent Crime Rates," Institute of Science, Technology, and Public Policy, Maharishi University of Management, April 14, 2016. https://doi.org/10.1177/2158244016637891.

263 The morphic resonance theory of Rupert Sheldrake, which claims the existence of an unknown type of telepathic interconnection within a species, is a possible explanation.

264 Larry Dossey, M.D., *Healing Words* (New York, NY: HarperOne, 1995). See also Richard Gerber, M.D., *Vibrational Medicine: New Choices for Healing Ourselves* (Santa Fe, NM: Bear & Co., 1998).

265 Peter Steinfels, "A Doctor Looks to Science for Proof of a Spiritual Realm," *New York Times*, December 19, 1993, Ideas and Trends, 14.

266 *The Jerusalem Bible: The New Testament*, 202.

267 Alice McDowell Pempel, "Spirituality of the Sky Gods: Women Christian Mystics," *Anima*, 5/2 (1979): 143-152.

268 McDowell Pempel, 148-9.

269 McDowell Pempel, 150.

270 van Stock and Dunlop, 80-81.

271 This story of Umar, Khalif of Arabia, appearing in Kahn, *Tales*, 115, illustrates the effect of this ability.

272 Kapleau, 311.

273 Kapleau, 311.

274 Khan, *Tales*, 69.

275 Buddhist Richard Baker writes of his teacher Shunryu Suzuki in the Introduction to *Zen Mind, Beginner's Mind*, 18.

276 Sikhar van Stolk writes of his teacher HIK in *Memories of a Sufi Sage*, 76.

277 Buber, 9.

278 Starr, 89.

279 Hafiz, *I Heard God Laughing*, 75.

References

Adyashanti. "The Great Expense of Darkness." Adyashanti, May 2019, Granlibakken Tahoe, 1 hr. 4 min. *Silent Retreat, Vol. 72 Talks*, CD or MP3. https://www.adyashanti.org/store/media/audio-downloads/1085.

Adyashanti. *Falling into Grace: Insights on the End of Suffering.* Boulder, CO: Sounds True, 2011.

Adyashanti. *The End of Your World: Uncensored Straight Talk on the Nature of Enlightenment.* Boulder, CO: Sounds True, 2008.

Adyashanti. *Emptiness Dancing.* Boulder, CO: Sounds True, 2006.

Alexander, Eben, M.D. *Proof of Heaven: A Neurosurgeon's Journey into the Afterlife.* New York: Simon & Schuster, 2012.

Alighieri, Dante. *The Divine Comedy: The Inferno, The Purgatorio, The Paradiso.* Translated by John Cardi. New York, NY: New American Library, 2003. John Cardi.

Allione, Lama Tsultrim, *Feeding Your Demons: Ancient Wisdom for Resolving Inner Conflict.* New York, NY: Little, Brown Spark, 2008.

Anderson, Sherry Ruth and Patricia Hopkins. *The Feminine Face of God: The Unfolding of the Sacred in Women.* New York, NY: Bantam Book, 1991.

Anodea Judith. *Eastern Body, Western Mind: Psychology and the Chakra System as a Path to the Self.* Berkley, CA: Celestial Arts, 1996.

Bacovcin, Helen. *The Way of a Pilgrim; And the Pilgrim Continues His Way: A New Translation.* Garden City, NY: Image Books, 1978.

Baker, Richard. Introduction to *Zen Mind, Beginner's Mind,* 13-18. Suzuki, Shunryu and Trudy Dixon. New York: Weatherhill, 1980.

Bancroft, Anne. *Weavers of Wisdom: Women Mystics of the Twentieth Century.* London: Arkana/Penguin, 1989.

Batchelor, Martine. "The Ten Oxherding Pictures," *Tricycle* (Spring 2000). https://tricycle.org/magazine/ten-oxherding-pictures/

Berceli, David *Trauma Releasing Exercises: A Revolutionary New Method for Stress/Trauma Recovery.* Charleston, SC: Book Surge Publishing, 2005.

Berry, Thomas. *The Sacred Universe: Earth, Spirituality, and Religion in the Twenty-First Century.* New York, NY: Columbia University Press, 2009.

Berry, Thomas. *The Dream of the Earth.* San Francisco, CA: Sierra Club Books, 1988.

The Bhagavad Gita. Translated by Juan Mascaró. New York, NY: Penguin Books, 1962.

Bob L. "The Second Step," *Mysterious Ways,* Aug/Sept 2019, 29.

Bourgeault, Cynthia. *Eye of the Heart: A Spiritual Journey into the Imaginal Realm.* Boulder, CO: Shambhala Publications, 2020.

Brennan, Gerald. *St. John of the Cross: His Life and Poetry.* Cambridge: Cambridge University Press, 1973.

Brunton, Paul. *The Notebooks of Paul Brunton: Perspectives.* Burdett, NY: Larson Publications, 1984.

Buber, Martin. *Hasidism and Modern Man.* Translated and edited by Maurice Friedman. Atlantic Highlands, New York: Humanities Press International, 1988, c. 1958.

Castaneda, Carlos. *The Eagle's Gift.* New York: Simon & Schuster, 1981.

Chödrön, Pema. *Welcoming the Unwelcome: Wholehearted Living in a Brokenhearted World.* Boulder, CO: Shambhala Publications, 2019.

DeMello, Anthony. https://www.demellospirituality.com/freedom/the-harder-you-try-to-change-the-worse-it-get/

Dillard, Annie. *Pilgrim at Tinker Creek.* New York: Harper's Magazine Press, 1974.

Dillbeck, Michael C. and Kenneth L. Cavanaugh. "Societal Violence and Collective Consciousness: Reduction of U.S. Homicide and Urban Violent Crime Rates." Institute of Science, Technology, and Public Policy, Maharishi University of Management. April 14, 2016. https://doi.org/10.1177/2158244016637891.

Dossey, Larry, M.D. *Healing Words.* New York, NY: HarperOne, 1995.

Eckenstein, Lina. *Woman Under Monasticism.* Cambridge: Cambridge University Press, 1896.

Egan, Harvey. *Christian Mysticism: The Future of a Tradition.* Eugene, OR: Wipf and Stock, 1998.

Eliade, Mircea. *The Two and the One.* Rutland, VT: Phoenix Books, 1979.

The Flower Ornament Scripture. Translated by Thomas Leary. Boulder, CO: Shambhala Publications, 1993.

Fox, Matthew. *Meditations with Meister Eckhart.* Rochester, NY: Bear & Company, 1983.

Fox, Matthew. *Illuminations of Hildegard of Bingen.* Rochester, VT: Bear & Company, 2003.

Freke, Timothy. *The Wisdom of the Sufi Sages.* Boston, MA: Godsfield Press, 1999.

Freke, Timothy. *The Wisdom of the Christian Mystics* Boston, MA: Godsfield Press, 1998.

Gangaji and Roslyn Moore. *Just Like You.* Mendocino, CA: Do Pub, 2003.

Gerber, Richard, M.D. *Vibrational Medicine: New Choices for Healing Ourselves.* Santa Fe, NM: Bear & Co., 1998.

Green, John Mark. *Johnmarkgreenpoetry.tumblr.com.* Nov. 8, 2015. https://johnmarkgreenpoetry.tumblr.com/post/132839955315/beautiful-are-those-whose-brokenness-gives-birth.

Gregorius Nyssenus, Everett Ferguson and Abraham J. Malherbe. *The Life of Moses*. New York: Paulist Press, 1978.

Hagelin, J. S., D. W. Orme-Johnson, M. Rainforth, K. Cavanaugh, C. N. Alexander, S. F. Shatkin, J. L. Davies, A. O. Hughs, and E. Ross. "Effects of Group Practice of the Transcendental Meditation Program on Preventing Violent Crime in Washington, D.C.: Results of the National Demonstration Project, June-July 1993." *Social Indicators Research* 47, no. 2 (1999):153-201.

Hafiz. *The Gift: Poems by Hafiz*. Translated by Daniel Ladinksy. New York, NY: Arkana, 1999.

Hafiz. *I Heard God Laughing: Renderings of Hafiz*. Translated by Daniel Ladinsky. Walnut Creek, CA: Sufism Reoriented, 1996.

Hafiz. *The Subject Tonight is Love: 60 Wild and Sweet Poems*. Translated by Daniel Ladinsky. Los Angeles: Pumpkin House Press, 1996.

Happold, F.C. *Mysticism: A Study and an Anthology*. Hammondsworth, Middlesex, England: Penguin Books, 1964.

Harvey, Andrew. *Teachings of the Christian Mystics*. Boulder, CO: Shambala, 2019.

Harvey, Andrew (Editor). *Teachings of Rumi*, Boulder, CO: Shambhala Publications, 1999

Hawken, Paul. *The Magic of Findhorn*. New York: Harper and Row, 1975.

Heimlich, Russell. "Mystical Experiences." Pew Research Center Fact-Tank. December 29, 2009. https://www.pewresearch.org/fact-tank/2009/12/29/mystical-experiences/

Helminski, Camille and Kabir. *Rumi Daylight: A Daybook of Spiritual Guidance*. Putney, VT: Threshold Books, 1990.

Helwa, A. *Secrets of Divine Love: A Spiritual Journey into the Heart of Islam*. Capistrano Beach, CA: Naulit Publishing House, 2020.

The Holy Bible. Revised Standard Edition. New York, NY: New

American Library, 1962.

Horowitz, Mikhail. *Illumination: The Saga of a Sufi Master.* New Lebanon, NY: Sacred Spirit Music, 2018.

Huxley, Aldous. "Visionary Experience." in *The Highest State of Consciousness*, edited by John White, 257-277. Garden City: Doubleday Anchor, 1972.

Inayat Khan, Pir Zia. *Mingled Waters: Sufism and the Mystical Unity of Religions.* New Lebanon, NY: Suluk Press, 2017.

Inayat Khan, Pir Vilayat, *Thinking Like the Universe: The Sufi Path of Awakening.* Edited by Pythia Peay. New York, NY: Thorsons, 2000.

Inayat Khan, Pir Vilayat. *Call of the Dervish.* Santa Fe, NM: Sufi Order Publications, 1981.

Inayat Khan, Pir Valayat. *The Message in Our Time: The Life and Teachings of Pir-O-Murshid Inayat Khan.* San Francisco, CA: Harper & Row, 1979.

John of the Cross. *Living Flame of Love.* Garden City, NY: Doubleday Image, 1962.

John of the Cross. *Spiritual Canticle.* Garden City, NY: Doubleday Image, 1961.

John of the Cross. *Dark Night of the Soul.* Garden City, NY: Doubleday Image, 1959.

John of the Cross. *Ascent of Mount Carmel.* Garden City, NY: Doubleday Image, 1958.

Johnson, Robert A. *Inner Work: Using Dreams and Imagination for Personal Growth.* San Francisco, CA: Harper & Row, 1986.

Jones, Alexander. *The Jerusalem Bible: The New Testament.* Garden City, NY: Doubleday, 1967.

Jones, Alexander. *The Jerusalem Bible.* Garden City, NY: Doubleday, 1966.

Julian of Norwich. *Julian of Norwich: Showings.* Translated by Edmund Colledge, O.S.A. and James Walsh, S. J. New York, NY: Paulist Press, 1978.

Jung, C. G. *Memories, Dreams, and Reflections*. New York, NY: Vintage Books, 1965.

Kapleau, Philip. *Three Pillars of Zen*. Boston, MA: Beacon Press, 1967.

Kennedy, Daniel Joseph. "St. Thomas Aquinas." In *Catholic Encyclopedia* 14, edited by Charles Herbermann. New York: Robert Appleton Company, 1912.

Khan, Hazrat Inayat. *The Complete Works of Pir-O-Murshid Hazrat Inayat Khan, Lectures on Sufism 1924 II: June 10-End of December*. New Lebanon, NY: Omega Publications, 2009.

Khan, Hazrat Inayat. *The Heart of Sufism*. Boston: Shambala Press, 1999.

Khan, Hazrat Inayat. *The Alchemy of Happiness*. London: East-West Publications, 1996.

Khan, Hazrat Inayat. *The Sufi Message of Hazrat Inayat Khan, Vol. XIII, The Gathas*. Katwijk, Holland: Published for International Headquarters Sufi Movement by Servire, 1982.

Khan, Hazrat Inayat. *Tales*. New Lebanon, NY: Omega Press, 1980.

Khan, Hazrat Inayat. *Gayan, Vadan, Nirtan*. Lebanon Springs, NY: Sufi Order Publications, 1980.

Khan, Hazrat Inayat. *Mastery Through Accomplishment*. New Lebanon, NY: Omega Press, 1978.

Khan, Hazrat Inayat. *The Complete Sayings of Hazrat Inayat Khan*. New Lebanon, NY: Sufi Order Publications, 1978.

Kornfield, Jack. *A Path with Heart*. New York: Bantam Books, 1993.

Lair, Jess. *I Don't Know Where I'm Going, But I Sure Ain't Lost*. Robbinsdale, MN: Fawcett Publications, 1983.

Lanzetta, Beverly. *The Monk Within: Embracing the Sacred Way of Life.* Sebastopol, CA: Blue Sapphire Books, 2018.

Lao Tsu, Gia-Fu Feng and Jane English. *Tao Te Ching.* New York, NY: Vintage Books, 1972.

Layman P'ang. *The Sayings of Layman P'ang: A Zen Classic of China.* Translated by James Green. Boulder, CO: Shambhala Publications, 2009.

Levine, Peter. *Waking the Tiger: Healing Trauma.* Berkeley, CA: North Atlantic Books, 1997.

Lowen, Alexander. *The Language of the* Body. New York, NY: Collier, 1971.

Ma, Anandamayi. *The Essential Sri Anandamayi Ma: Life and Teachings of a 20th century Indian Saint.* Edited by Joseph A. Fitzgerald. Bloomington, IN: World Wisdom, 2007.

Maa, Amoda. *Falling Open in a World Falling Apart: The Essential Teaching Amoda Maa.* Burdett, NY: Larson Publications, 2020.

Maa, Amoda. Retreat at Treman Center, Ithaca, NY. April 27-28, 2019.

Maloney, George A., S. J. *Prayer of the Heart.* Notre Dame, IN: Ave Maria Press, 1995.

Maloney, George A., S. J. *Called to Intimacy: Living in the Indwelling Presence.* Staten Island, NY: Alba House, 1983.

Maloney, George A., S. J. *The Everlasting Now: Meditations on the Mysteries of Life and Death as They Touch Us in Our Daily Choices.* Notre Dame, IN: Ave Maria Press, 1980.

Mauryani, Takao. "Buddha's Supernatural Powers in the Lotus Sutra," https://core.ac.uk/download/pdf/148766201.pdf

McDowell, Alice. "Altered States of Consciousness and Mystical Experience: A Topology of Inner Space." Doctoral thesis, Fordham University, 1971.

McDowell Pempel, Alice. "Spirituality of the Sky Gods: Women Christian Mystics." *Anima,* 5/2 (1979): 143-152.

McDowell, Alice. *Hidden Treasure: How to Break Free of Five*

Patterns that Hide Your True Self. Berkeley, CA: She Writes Press, 2017.

McLaughlin, Corrine. "Tuning into the Best Channel." *New Realities*, July/August 1987, 37-42.

Meister Eckhart, *The Essential Sermons, Commentaries, Treatises and Defense.* Translated and edited by Bernard McGinn and Edmund Colledge. New York: Paulist Press, 1981.

Menzies, Lucy. *The Revelations of Mechthild of Magdeburg.* London: Longmans, Green & Co., 1953.

Merton, Thomas. *New Seeds of Contemplation.* New York, NY: New Directions, 1972.

Merton, Thomas. *The Way of Chuang Tzu.* Boulder, CO: Shambhala Publications, 2004.

Moody, Raymond. *Reflections on Life After Life.* New York: Bantam Books, 1977.

Moody, Raymond. *Life After Life*, New York: Bantam Books, 1975.

Nagarjuna. *The Treatise on the Great Perfection of Wisdom* http://the-wanderling.com/siddhis.html.

Nietzke, Anne. "The Miracle of Elisabeth Kubler-Ross." *Cosmopolitan.* February 1980, 211.

Nolan, J. Paddy, dir. *Seeing is Believing.* Season 1, Episode 1, "Pray, Hope and Don't Worry: A Celebration of Padre Pio," aired in 1989, JPN Film Services Production.

Paumgarten, Nick. "The Descent of Man." *The New Yorker.* April 29, 2019, 48-57.

Peck, Scott. *The Road Less Traveled.* New York: Simon & Schuster, 1978.

Pierrakos, John. *Core Energetics: Developing the Capacity to Love and Heal.* Mendocino, CA: Life Rhythms Publications, 1990.

Prabhavananda, Swami and Frederick A. Manchester. *The Upanishads: Breadth of the Eternal: The Principal Texts.* New York, NY:

New American Library, 1957.

Red Pine, Translated. *The Heart Sutra*. Berkeley, CA: Counterpoint Press, 2004.

Reich, Wilhelm. *Character Analysis*, translated by Theodore P. Wolfe. New York, NY: Farrar & Straus, 1971.

Reinhold, Hans Ansgar, Editor. *The Soul Afire: Revelation of the Mystics*. NY: Doubleday Images, 1973.

Reps, Paul and Nyogen Senzaki. *Zen Flesh, Zen Bones: A Collection of Zen and Pre-Zen Writings*. Rutledge, VT: Tuttle Publications, 1985, c. 1957.

Sabbath, Linda. *The Radiant Heart*. Denville, NJ: Dimension Books, 1977.

Seabrook, Elizabeth M., Margaret L. Kern, Nikki S. Rickard. "Social Networking Sites, Depression, and Anxiety: A Systematic Review." *JMIR Mental Health* 3, no. 4 (2016): e50. https://mental.jmir.org/2016/4/e50/.

Seinfeld, Jerry. "Everything You Need to know About Parenting from 8 Jerry Seinfeld Quotes," *Fatherly.com*, June 4, 2015. https://www.fatherly.com/love-money/everything-you-need-to-know-about-parenting-from-8-jerry-seinfeld-quotes/.

Shah, Idries. *The Way of the Sufi*. New York: E.P. Dutton. 1970.

Smith, Huston. *The World Religions: Our Great Wisdom Traditions*. San Francisco, HarperCollins, 1991.

Soseki, Muso. *Dialogues in a Dream: The Life and Zen Teaching of Muso Soseki*. Translated and edited by Thomas Yuho Kirchner. Sommerville, MA: Wisdom Publications, 2015.

Starr, Mirabai. *Wild Mercy: Living the Fierce and Tender Wisdom of the Women Mystics*. Boulder, CO: Sounds True, 2019.

Steinfels, Peter. "A Doctor Looks to Science for Proof of a Spiritual Realm." *New York Times*, December 19, 1993, Ideas and Trends, 14.

Suzuki, Daisetz Teitaro. *Japanese and Zen Culture*. New York,

NY: Bollingen Foundation, 1959.

Suzuki, Daisetz Teitaro. *Mysticism: Christian and Buddhist*. New York, NY: Collier Books, 1957.

Teilhard de Chardin, Pierre. *Hymn of the Universe*. New York: Harper & Row, 1961.

Teresa of Ávila. *Interior Castle*. Mineola, NY: Dover Publications, 2007.

Teresa of Ávila. *The Life of St. Teresa of Ávila*. Translated by Alice Lady Lovat. London: Herbert & Daniel, 1912.

Teresa of Ávila. *Book of the Foundations*. Translated by Rev. John Dalton. London: T. Jones, 1853.

Theophane the Monk. *Tales of a Magic Monastery*. Reno, NV: Crossroad, 2010.

Thérèse of Lisieux. *Story of a Soul*. Charlotte, NC: Saint Benedict Press, TAN Books, 2010.

Thompson, Augustine, O. P. *Francis of Assisi: A New Biography*. Ithaca, NY: Cornell University Press, 2012.

Thurman, Howard. "The Sound of the Genuine." March 12, 1980. *Expanding Common Ground: The Howard Thurman & Sue Bailey Thurman Collections at Boston University*, 41:53, http://archives.bu.edu/web/howard-thurman/virtual-listening-room/detail?id=360318.

Twenge, Jean M., A. Bell Cooper, Thomas E. Joiner, and Mary E. Duffy. "Age, Period, and Cohort Trends in Mood Disorder Indicators and Suicide-Related outcomes in a Nationally Representative Dataset, 2005-2017." *Journal of Abnormal Psychology* 128, no. 3, (2019): 185-199. http://dx.doi.org/10.1037/abn0000410

Underhill, Evelyn. *Mysticism: A Study in the Nature and Development of Man's Spiritual Consciousness*. New York, E.P. Dutton, 1961.

Unset, Sigrid. *Catherine of Siena*. New York, NY: Sheed & Ward, 1954.

van den Dungen, Wim. *Ten Ox-Herding Images: Training the Mind for Enlightenment*. Brasschaat, Belgium: Taurus Press, 2018.

Van der Kolk, M.D., Bessel. *The Body Keeps the Score*. New York, NY: Penguin Books, 2014.

Van Stolk, Sirkar and Daphne Dunlop. *Memories of a Sufi Sage: Hazrat Inayat Khan*. The Hague; East-West Publications Fonds B.V., 1967.

de Vitray-Meyerovitch, Eva. *Rumi and Sufism*. Translation Simone Fattal. Sausalito, CA: The Post-Apollo Press, 1987.

Wautier d'Aygalliers, Alfred and Fred Rothwell. *Ruysbroeck the Admirable*. London: J.M. Dent & Sons, 1925.

White, John. *The Highest State of Consciousness*. Garden City, NY: Doubleday Anchor Books, 1972.

Whitehead, Alfred North. *Science and the Modern World*. New York, NY: Free Press, 1977 c. 1925.

Yogananda, Paramahansa. *Autobiography of a Yogi*. Los Angeles: Self-Realization Fellowship, 1977.

Further Reading

Adyashanti, *Resurrecting Jesus: Embodying the Spirit of a Revolutionary Mystic.* Boulder, CO: Sounds True, 2014.

Adyashanti. *The Impact of Awakening: Excerpts from the Teachings of Adyashanti.* San Jose, CA. Open Gate Publishing, 2000.

Bourgeault, Cynthia. *Wisdom Jesus: Transforming Heart and Mind—A New Perspective on Christ and His Message.* Boston: Shambhala Press, 2008.

Bourgeault, Cynthia. *The Wisdom Way of Knowing: Reclaiming an Ancient Tradition to Awaken the Heart.* San Francisco, CA: Jossey Bass, 2003.

Bucke, R. C. *Cosmic Consciousness: A Study in the Evolution of the Human Mind.* Second edition, reprint of 1905 original. Eastford, CT: Martino Publishing, 2010.

Chittister, Joan. *The Gift of Years: Growing Older Gracefully.* Katonah, NY: BlueBridge, 2008.

Chittister, Joan, *Illuminated Life: Monastic Wisdom for Seekers of Light.* Maryknoll, NY: Orbis Books, 2000.

Fields, Rick. *Chop Wood, Carry Water: A Guide to Finding Spiritual Fulfillment in Everyday Life.* Los Angeles: Jeremy P. Tarcher, 1984.

Inayat Khan, Pir Vilayat. *The Ecstasy Beyond Knowing: A Manual of Meditation.* New Lebanon, NY: Suluk Press, 2014.

Khan, Hazrat Inayat. *The Inner Life*. Boston: Shambala Press, 1997.

Khan, Hazrat Inayat. *The Sufi Message of Hazrat Inayat Khan, Vol. VIII, The Art of Being.* Rockport, MA: Element, Inc. 1991.

Koller, John M. "Ox-herding: Stages of Zen Practice." 2004. http://www.columbia.edu/cu/weai/exeas/resources/oxherding.html.

Maa, Amoda. *Embodied Enlightenment: Living Your Awakening in Every Moment.* Oakland, CA: Reveal Press, 2017.

Peace Pilgrim. *Peace Pilgrim: Her Life and Works in Her Own Words*. Santa Fe, NM: Ocean Tree Books, 1982.

Rohr, Richard. *Falling Upward: A Spirituality for the Two Halves of Life*. San Francisco, CA: Jossey-Bass, 2011.

Rohr, Richard. *The Naked Now: Learning to See as the Mystics See.* New York: The Crossroad Publishing Company, 2009.

Schmid, Tanya. *Tanya's Collection of Zen Stories*. Self-published, 2018.

Senzaki, Nyogen, and Ruth McCandless. *Buddhism and Zen.* New York: Philosophical Library, 1953.

Shah, Idries. *Tales of the Dervishes*. New York: E.P. Dutton. 1970.

Steindl-Rast, Br. David, *i am through you so i.* New York, NY: Paulist Press, 2017.

Acknowledgements

My heart opens wide whenever I think of all the people who helped birth *Dance of Light*. I want to thank my friend and colleague, Julie Schnepel, the first person to read my writing and add her comments and editing expertise. She always made the text better.

My book writing coach, Lisa Tener, valiantly contributed to the overall direction of the book. After reading the first draft, she asked if I wanted the book to be academic or trade since it veered toward the academic side. I told her trade because I wanted *Dance of Light* to be accessible to as many people who would benefit from its contents as possible. She suggested I address the reader personally and advised me to break up the manuscript by adding boxes filled with stories, tales, and poetry from the different wisdom traditions.

Lisa did not like the original title, *Wisdom's Way*. Finding the right title—an important enticement to readers—proved to be a long and difficult task. Nothing seemed to fit. One Thanksgiving, one of my sons, Sean, his wife Trisha, and their three kids brainstormed about the title. I loved how the three generations came together. We decided on *Dimensions of Light*, but Lisa felt it was too mathematical. Knowing my frustration with the title, Lynne Lagarde, my dear friend and fellow companion on the spiritual path since graduate school, offered a list of possibilities using the term light. We both zeroed in on *Dance of Light* as the right title. Finally, a solution! This title saga is just one example of the challenges—along with the joys—of book writing and the crucial help others give for the best possible outcome.

I'm grateful to all those who read the first drafts and gave comments, asked for clarification, or commented on its theology. Lynne and I had fun with Marilyn McNamara, another dear friend from graduate school, discussing and challenging the ideas appearing in *Dance of Light*. My appreciative heart also goes out to those early readers who gave their professional insights: Bill Barnard, Jalaja Bonheim, Meghan Don, Peter Fortunato, Mary Gilliland, Kelly Malone, Maureen O'Brien, Varia Siegel, and of course, my Sufi spiritual leader, Pir Zia Inayat Khan.

I'm eternally grateful for Jill Swenson, my developmental editor and agent, for holding my hand through the vicissitudes of writing a proposal and finding a publisher. I loved how she quickly answered my emails—a trait that always gave me needed assurance and one I value in working extensively with anyone. Her comprehensive knowledge of the book publishing world, her editing and formatting skills, and her sensitivity astound me. I know I can rely on her for any of my questions and consider her a heart-felt friend.

I'm very pleased to partner with Wisdom Editions for the publication of *Dance of Light*. Publishers Ian Leask and Gary Lindenberg are spiritual seekers themselves and have the knowledge and expertise to deliver my book to readers. Their enthusiasm for *Dance of Light* encourages and excites me. It's a pleasure working with them. I was amazed to discover that Gary designs book covers in addition to editing. He reads a manuscript first and waits for an image to emerge from what he has read. I love his design for *Dance of Light* and how he collaborated with my son, Sean, to perfect its finer details.

I devoured Kyriacos Markides' books early in my teaching career and was pleased to meet him when he came to Ithaca in the 90s. We lost touch for many years until I received his email announcing his latest book, *The Accidental Immigrant*. I knew he'd be an excellent person to ask to review *Dance of Light*. His enthusiasm prompted me to inquire if he would write the book's Foreward and he graciously accepted. He is a beautiful, kind, intelligent and humble human being. Thank you, Kyriacos!

So much of my spiritual knowledge and personal experiences have come from retreats that I want to thank those who guided me during those times: Aziza Scott, Mahdiah Jacobs-Kahn, Pir Vilayat Khan, Pir Zia Inayat Khan and Adyashanti. I also want to recognize the retreat centers that hosted these retreats: Light on the Hill Retreat

Center, Mt. Savior Monastery, Transfiguration Monastery, The Abode of the Message, and Omega Institute.

My dear husband, Larry Muscat, deserves numerous thanks for calmly listening to the ups and downs of the writing process, shopping for food and cooking meals so I could spend time concentrating on book writing. He is my human anchor.

I honor the Great Source of All and the mystics past and present whose inspiring words and actions furthered me along the path. I hope they will enkindle in you the same desire to continue on this awesome journey.

About the Author

Alice McDowell, Ph.D., is an author, spiritual director, workshop leader, retreat guide and founder of the Hidden Treasure Program—a three-year training in personal and spiritual growth. She co-founded Light on the Hill Retreat Center in 1991 where she continues to guide individuals and groups on their spiritual journeys. She is author of *Hidden Treasure: How to Break Free of Five Patterns that Hide Your True Self* (She Writes Press, 2017). As a professor of religious studies at Ithaca College for eighteen years, she taught courses in mysticism, world religions, depth psychology, and women's studies, and received the Dana Fellow for Excellence in College Teaching. McDowell has a Ph.D. in theology from Fordham University and has trained with Sufi and Buddhist teachers, Christian contemplatives, and humanistic and transpersonal psychologists. She is a mother of two, the grandmother of four, and lives at Light on the Hill Retreat Center in Van Etten, NY, with her husband and two cats.

Visit her at: www.alicemcdowellauthor.com

CPSIA information can be obtained
at www.ICGtesting.com
Printed in the USA
BVHW072135130123
656272BV00007B/327